D1636826

DEADLINE

ABOUT THE BOOK

You will meet many interesting people in this book. One of them is the author, Kathy Begley. Though young to write her autobiography, she has completed at least volume one in *Deadline*. This is the story—*her* story—of a young woman who was determined to become a good newspaper reporter.

It tells how she did it. Like most news reporters, her personal life became intertwined with her professional life. She wrote her mother's obituary. She celebrated a birthday in a police station. She fell in love at a gubernatorial election headquarters.

Though not as famous as the reporters who broke the Watergate story, Kathy Begley here writes a true account that goes beyond journalism. This is the story of how wisdom and maturity come to a young woman who does not want history to pass her by.

DEADLINE

Kathleen A. Begley

G. P. Putnam's Sons -- New York

LIBRARY OF CONGRESS CATALOGING IN PUBLICATION DATA
Begley, Kathleen A   Deadline.
Autobiographical. Includes index.
SUMMARY: The author relates how she came to be a
news reporter and her early experiences on the job.
1. Begley, Kathleen A. 2. Journalists—United
States—Biography—Juvenile literature. [1. Begley,
Kathleen A. 2. Journalists] I. Title.
PN4874.B364A33 070.92′4 [B] [92] 77-2550
ISBN 0-399-20611-6

TO WILEY,
WHO SHARES MY JOY

Preface

Ten years ago, when I became a newspaper reporter, the trade offered a certain sense of excitement but lacked much semblance of professional prestige. For a woman the job was a never-ending battle against being pigeon-holed into writing solely about weddings and engagements. Watergate and the feminist movement created substantial changes. Reporters, some of them women, suddenly became national folk heroes. As one editor's wife recently put it, "Journalism is the Peace Corps of the 1970s."

To be sure, interest in the news media has increased dramatically in recent years. Enrollment in journalism schools has more than doubled since the late 1960s. Newspaper-related books have skyrocketed to the top of the best-seller lists. Many magazines now devote entire sections to articles on "The Press."

For the past decade I have had an insider's view of the workings of daily American newspapers, including the Pulitzer Prize-winning Philadelphia *Inquirer*. Like most reporters, my personal life often has been intertwined with my professional life: I wrote my mother's obituary, I celebrated my birthday in a police station, I fell in love at a gubernatorial election headquarters.

Unlike the recent work of Washington *Post* reporters Carl Bernstein and Bob Woodward, my career focused not on a single story but on a myriad stories that took me all over the country. Certainly, newspapering often poses ethical problems that I never quite resolved. But it also provides a young person with an intimate look at some of the world's most fascinating people, places, and events.

I'm glad I've had a ringside view.

KATHLEEN A. BEGLEY

DEADLINE

1 -- The Beginning

The policeman walked into the city room and said that "a little girl" injured in a car accident had asked him to bring a photograph to the newspaper office.

"She was lying on the street holding this picture in her hand," the policeman told the startled newspaper editor. "So I thought I better bring it over and check with you."

The "little girl" trying so anxiously to meet her first deadline back in 1966 was I, then a naïve, eighteen-year-old college student. A summer copygirl at the Delaware County *Daily Times* in Chester, Pennsylvania, I had been sent by the editors to pick up a picture and get some obituary information on a young soldier in our coverage area who had been killed in Vietnam. It was the beginning of the peak war effort and each death still was Big News. Later, as the conflict wore on, the obituaries of casualties gradually became smaller and smaller so that newspapers could fit them all in.

Although I soon would learn that death plays a key role in many stories, this was my first experience with a grief-stricken family. As I asked the sobbing mother to give me the exact spelling of her son's first name and a list of his high-school accomplishments, I felt extremely uncomfortable having to bother with journalistic details at such a tragic time. As a fledgling newspaperwoman, I knew that asking pertinent questions was my job; as a human being, however, I knew that answering the questions was placing an additional emotional strain on an already severely strained family.

It is a conflict I never quite resolved during subsequent years of interviewing survivors and victims of hundreds of tragedies. Later in my career I often tried to mask my discomfort at such assignments by joking to editors that I always told bereaved families that the exact same misfortune, including my own suicide, had happened to me. But, in reality, I always was a jumble of emotion in these situations, madly taking notes with one hand, sadly wiping away a tear with the other.

At the end of my conversation with the mother of the Vietnam casualty, she began crying so hard that her shoulders shook violently and her breath came in loud gasps. I gave up all pretense of objectivity; I began crying too. Before making a hasty exit, I scribbled down the name of the funeral director who was arranging services for the dead serviceman. I deliberately didn't ask his address because I didn't want to upset the family any further. But as I walked out the door, I said a silent prayer that he would be listed under the "mortician" heading in the telephone book.

Back in my car, a ten-year-old jalopy that I just had bought for seventy-five dollars, I suddenly realized that I had only a half-hour to get back to the city room. Although this was my initial outside assignment, I knew enough about newspapering by then to know that getting the story in on time was vitally important. So I certainly didn't want to miss my first deadline.

Unfortunately, I was concentrating so much on my wristwatch that I didn't bother to concentrate at all on my driving. As I approached a large intersection about a half-mile from the *Daily Times*, I checked the time again and was alarmed to find it was now 8:45 A.M., just fifteen minutes until deadline. And there I was, stuck in a left-hand lane waiting for a long row of oncoming cars to go by before I could turn on the green light.

By the time all of the other cars had passed, which seemed an eternity, the traffic signal flashed to amber. I knew I didn't have time to sit through another red light. So I panicked. Instead of completing my turn, which would have been permissible since I had been waiting for oncoming cars, I plowed up on the curb, along the sidewalk, and onto a nearby church lawn. I was brought to a dramatic halt by a large oak tree.

In the silence that followed the crash, as sometimes happens to me in moments of crisis, I perceived the scene as if I were watching myself in a movie. In the distance a group of people were staring in horror out the window of a diner, their forks still in midair. A little kid walked by the wreckage, looked in at me, and started screaming. A police light began revolving in the rearview mirror. I was scared to death that THE END would appear on my mental movie screen at any minute.

Fortunately, the accident wasn't nearly so serious as it looked. Upon impact with the tree, my car had tipped over on its left side so that the only thing visible to onlookers was my head. I didn't realize it at the time, but my mouth was bleeding profusely and my face was severely bruised. But I felt absolutely no pain. My main problem was that I couldn't get out of the car because the door was pressed firmly against the ground.

When the ambulance arrived, the attendants lifted me

through the passenger window and placed me gingerly on the pavement. Somehow, moments before the crash, I had managed to grab the dead serviceman's picture and I still was clutching it in my left hand. I knew that I wasn't in any condition to deliver it to the city room in person, so I beseeched a nearby policeman to carry out my mission.

"Take this picture to the *Daily Times,*" I pleaded.

At the hospital, the doctors discovered that the blood from my mouth was not the result of internal injuries as they had feared but the result of deeply cut gums. My front teeth also had cracked when my chin hit the steering wheel, but amazingly, they hadn't broken off. The most serious damage was to the bones in my right hand, which had splintered into many pieces.

As the doctors were consulting one another in hushed, mumbled tones, my mother came rushing into the emergency room. She told me that there wasn't a thing to worry about, that the nurses told her over the phone that I would be just fine, that everything would work out for the best. Then, when she thought I wasn't looking, my mother pulled some smelling salts out of her purse and took a quick whiff.

"Where did you get that?" I asked, rather amused at the sight of my mother sniffing anything stronger than perfume.

"Oh, I've carried this around for years," she said a bit sheepishly. "I don't want to faint in an emergency."

Just then, one of the doctors interrupted to announce that I would have to go to the operating room to have my hand set. Before I had a chance to think about it, an orderly whisked me down the hallway. At first the doctors tried to line up the bones without cutting the skin or giving me anesthesia. I tried to take my mind off the sudden pain by counting all the lights in the brightly lit ceiling. Then one of the broken bones scraped against a nerve and pain shot up the entire length of my arm. I passed out. An anesthesiologist threw a mask over my face and another doctor reached for a scalpel.

That night, Joe Jennings, then associate editor of the *Daily Times*, visited me at the hospital. He was carrying a late edition of the paper. Although I still was groggy from the anesthesia, I was conscious enough to look for the serviceman's photograph. It was not there. My spirits sank.

Noticing my obvious disappointment, Joe comforted me by emphasizing that the picture had, in fact, arrived in time for deadline. But the editors had decided at the last minute not to use it so that they could fit in a late-breaking story. Joe pointed to a three-paragraph article on the back page of the front section:

> Kathleen A. Begley, 18, of 412 Bickley Place, was injured this morning when her car struck a tree at 9th and Butler Sts.
>
> Miss Begley was detained at Crozer Chester Medical Center with a cut lip and bruises of the right hand and both legs.
>
> A Daily Times employe, Miss Begley was returning from an assignment in Aston when the accident occurred about 9 a.m. Franklin Rescue Squad took her to the hospital.

Although the details of my injuries were not quite accurate, because the story was written before my condition was fully diagnosed, I was ecstatic to see my name in the paper. Years later, I often would joke that I had become a reporter primarily to get over an identity crisis. Most reporters readily admit that the state of their ego is directly related to the number of times their name has appeared in print lately: the higher the number, the higher the spirits.

The day following the accident, Arthur Mayhew, then city editor of the *Daily Times*, telephoned to see how I was feeling. By then I was unhappily aware that I was going to be out of circulation—newspaper or otherwise—for quite some time. Before the crash, my family doctor had been urging me to have a benign tumor removed from my left leg. I kept putting it off. But now, since I was flat on my back anyway, I told the doctor to go ahead. I figured that I would have to delay returning to college until the second semester in January.

Arthur tried to cheer me up. His technique was excellent.

"Look, when you get back on your feet, you can be a full-fledged reporter until you go back to school," he said.

Arthur's promise was all I needed to make one of the speediest recoveries in history. I didn't want him to forget about me. Within a week of the surgery on my leg, I was back in the city room, developing a special seven-finger typing technique that used my left hand and the only two fingers sticking out of the cast on my right hand. But I didn't mind. Although I had taken a touch-typing course in high school, back in the days when all young girls were told they'd never get a job without secretarial skills, I was always a miserable typist. Eliminating three fingers didn't harm my typing a bit.

Although my accident was the fortunate stroke of misfortune that began my formal journalism career, I had been interested in writing for quite some time. In third grade I remember beaming with pride when the teacher hung up my composition on the circus. In sixth grade I started a class newsletter. In eighth grade I wrote my first book of poems. So when grown-ups started asking me what I wanted to be when I grew up, I started replying, "A newspaper reporter." I figured that earning money for writing had to be one of the best of all possible worlds. I still do.

Luckily, my high-school journalism teacher was a Roman Catholic nun, Sister Marie Dolores, who was infinitely more street-wise than many professional journalists out on the streets. In my junior year Sister somehow charmed and cajoled the school financial department into sponsoring six students on a month-long journalism program at Catholic University in Washington, D.C. I was one of them. The following year, I won first prize in a high-school press tournament sponsored by Temple University in Philadelphia.

So, when I obtained the summer job as a copygirl at the *Daily Times*, I was eager to show the boss that I already knew the basics of newswriting, which essentially is to cram the "who-what-when-where-why" into the first paragraph or two of every news story. The idea is that hurried readers will be able to get the gist of the news quickly and concisely.

The boss I most wanted to impress was Arthur. But he really intimidated me. Although Arthur wasn't yet thirty years old at that time, he was clearly in full control of the newsroom, often working ten to twelve hours a day. Every morning, he would show up about 6 A.M. and work until the late afternoon. In the four years I worked at the *Daily Times*, I don't remember Arthur's ever taking a break for lunch. As far as I could see, his only diversions were cellophane-wrapped packages of peanut butter and crackers, which I hate; strong coffee, which I loathe; and big cigars, which I despise. Yet I loved Arthur and I wanted desperately for him just to like me.

After I had worked about a month as a copygirl, which consisted mainly of going for paper, coffee, and sandwiches, I decided to try to demonstrate my journalistic talents. I began writing Arthur notes like this:

> Kathleen A. Begley (who), a summer copygirl at the Delaware County Daily Times, announced today (when) in the city room (where) that she would like to become a newspaper reporter (what).
>
> "I've wanted to be a reporter for a long time (why)," Miss Begley said. "I would work very hard."

To this day, I am not quite sure whether it was my initiative before my car accident or Arthur's sympathy for me afterward that prompted him to offer the reporting job while I was still in the hospital. I suspect it was a combination.

One of my first feature stories was a color advance on the city's annual parade honoring Casimir Pulaski, a Polish soldier who fought in the U.S. Revolutionary War. Before large events such as parades, newspapers frequently print bright behind-the-scenes stories to create reader interest in the upcoming event. My assignment was to interview an elderly Polish woman who had been sewing elaborate ethnic costumes for the marchers for more than twenty-five years. It wasn't a wildly exciting topic perhaps, but I was wildly excited.

"Ah, who cares about a little old lady making costumes?" a friend of mine asked when I told him about the interview.

"I bet a lot of people do," I said defensively.

"Well, I think it's stupid," he said. "Nobody is going to read it anyway; everyone gets their news on television in this day and age."

Not in my family. My earliest memories of my mother are of her sitting up late at night in the living room, devouring every word in the evening newspaper. A native of Ireland, she virtually educated herself through reading. So when I began writing professionally, she naturally became my biggest fan, holding me in even greater esteem than her two favorites, Drew Pearson and Art Buchwald. To this day, my mother is the only person I've ever known who always read the editorial page first. And that includes editorial writers.

After my full recovery from my car mishap, I had become so infatuated with the newspaper business that I couldn't bear the idea of quitting my job and returning to Duquesne University in Pittsburgh, Pennsylvania, about three hundred miles from the *Daily Times*. It would be a long commute. So I decided to transfer to Widener College in Chester and later to Temple University in Philadelphia, so that I could continue as a reporter. Although this decision meant that I would be both working and attending classes full-time, my parents heartily approved. My father, who had arrived in the United States from Ireland at the height of the Depression, used to get tears in his eyes every time my name—half of which, of course, was the same as his—appeared in the paper. He frequently bought five or ten extra copies to send to his relatives in County Donegal, giving the *Daily Times* an unexpected international circulation.

To many of my peers, however, who didn't realize that I was sandwiching a full load of classes between work hours, I was labeled a "college dropout." When I didn't return to Duquesne, a lot of people nodded disapprovingly that I had thrown away a college scholarship. I didn't care. I couldn't have been prouder if the *Times* had been the prestigious New York version rather than the small-town Delaware County daily.

As it turned out, my decision to work during college gave me a keen advantage several years later when the job market was flooded with thousands of eager young journalism graduates. Like them, I had a college degree. But, in addition, I had that special quality that works such magic in the job market: experience.

In the middle of my junior year, when I had been working for a year and a half, my editor urged me to enter a contest sponsored by the local chapter of Sigma Delta Chi, a national journalism society. The entry consisted of an essay, clippings, academic record, and recommendations. I chuckled when I read one of the paragraphs in a letter written by Thomas D. Davis, then executive editor of the *Daily Times*: "We value Miss Begley so highly that we have rearranged her work schedule several times so that she can continue her education."

Ah, I thought, at least Mr. Davis didn't think I was a college dropout. Thinking of how many times he had juggled my hours, I bet he sometimes wished I was.

Much to my surprise, I won the contest and received a five-hundred-dollar scholarship. A month or so later, I found out about a similar competition sponsored by the Newspaper Fund of America, a foundation set up to aid journalism students. Because the fund's contest was on a national level, I didn't think I had much of a chance of winning. But my mother, who now predicted a future for me as glamorous as Brenda Starr's, felt that I did. So I entered. And then quickly forgot about it.

During the early part of that summer, the headlines

were filled with stories about Richard Nixon's planned political comeback and Eugene McCarthy's philosophical attempt to gain the presidency. It was 1968 and the country was torn with grief at the seemingly never-ending torment of Vietnam. My mother, who liked McCarthy's position against the war almost as much as his Irish last name, decided to campaign actively for the first time in her life. As she canvassed the neighborhood for signatures on pro-McCarthy petitions, I marveled at her participation in a movement composed primarily of young people half her age. Because of my feelings that newspaper reporters should remain objective during political disputes, I didn't campaign at all. But I secretly cheered my mother on.

On the weekend of the Republican National Convention, I was cohostess at a farewell party for a reporter who recently had resigned. My parents were planning to attend a bon-voyage buffet for a family friend who was returning to Ireland. It was August 3, 1974, a long, hot, summer's day. Before leaving for my party, I set my mother's hair and told her to have a good time. She told me to be home early, which made me furious because I was a sophisticated twenty-year-old newspaper reporter, and so I left in a huff.

Before returning home, however, I gathered together a peace offering: six quarts of leftover ginger ale, a beverage which my mother drank every night as she embroidered at the dining-room table. When I got back to our apartment, where we had moved just a few months earlier, I was surprised to discover that my parents hadn't gotten back yet. I checked the kitchen clock and noted that it was almost 1 A.M. Hmmph, I thought to myself, and she told me to be home early.

Figuring that I'd jokingly tell my mother that she

wouldn't be allowed out for a week for missing her curfew, I sat down on the sofa, slipped off my shoes, and began to leaf through the current issue of *Newsweek*. But I couldn't seem to concentrate on anything but the brief Newsmakers feature that appears in the middle of the magazine. So I picked up an issue of *Glamour* and started looking at the new fall fashions. As I glanced over an assortment of wool miniskirts, the telephone rang. It was a few minutes before 2 A.M.

The voice on the other end of the line identified herself as a nurse at a hospital about ten miles away.

"Your parents have been in an accident," she said.

I gripped the receiver tighter. My heart beat frantically. My mouth went completely dry. For a moment, I couldn't think of a single thing to say.

Then, acting on a delayed reflex, I began barreling out questions as if I were on an assignment.

"Where did it happen? Who was involved? What time was it?"

After a pause, I repeated a phrase I had used so often while reporting on accident stories, "What are their conditions—is anyone critical?"

The nurse did not give me a single direct answer. Suddenly, I no longer felt like the confident newspaper reporter. Instead, I felt once again like the helpless little girl who used to dream, as most children do, that her parents had abandoned her.

"What . . . what should I do?" I asked the nurse. "I . . . I mean are my parents on their way home . . . or should I come to the hospital?"

"Oh, by all means come," she said.

After hanging up, I quickly put on my shoes and ran downstairs from our second-floor apartment. As I searched inside my purse for the car keys, I suddenly thought of a horrible irony: neither of my parents drove an automobile and neither of them liked riding in one. Although I had recently purchased a new car to replace the one I had wrecked, my mother had gotten inside of it only once; but she got out of it very quickly when she saw that I had intentions of starting it up.

After finding the car keys, I realized that I had no idea how to get to the hospital. Frantic, I ran up to the corner of the tree-lined street in an attempt to get a neighbor or a passing motorist to help. But no one was around. The only lights on the street were coming from our living room; I had forgotten to turn them off.

I ran back upstairs, taking the steps two at a time, and called the hospital.

"Look, can you send someone for me?" I asked, my voice breaking. "I don't know how to get there."

"I'm afraid we don't have anyone to pick you up," the nurse replied. "Why don't you call the police?"

When I followed her advice, the local Ridley Park, Pennsylvania, police told me that they couldn't cross municipal lines in noncrime cases. But, they added, they could relay me from police car to police car if I wanted.

I wanted. "Please, just come," I said, my voice breaking.

As I waited for the patrol car to arrive, I tried to call my older sister, Mary. I knew that she and her husband, Albert, had driven my parents to the bon-voyage party. I got no answer and I imagined my sister's body lying in the wreckage somewhere where the police hadn't noticed it.

By the time the patrol car arrived, I had bitten off all of my fingernails and shredded my headscarf into pieces. I asked the policeman if he had heard anything about my parents' accident. He said he hadn't. When we got to the border of Ridley Park, a Morton police car was waiting. I asked him also if he had heard anything about the accident. He said he had no information either. He soon relayed me to a third car in Springfield.

As we approached a nearby shopping center, I could see in the distance the glaring lights of a police wagon and the wreckage of a car smashed against a utility pole. At the same time, a loud voice boomed over the police radio, "The coroner is on his way to the hospital."

I did not bother to ask the third policeman any questions. From my reporting experience I knew that the coroner's involvement meant only one thing: someone was dead. And I knew in my heart who it was.

"My mother is dead," I told the policeman in an eerie, matter-of-fact voice.

I was right.

As I walked into the gleaming white hospital emergency room, a nurse walked up and told me my mother "hadn't made it." The nurse then hugged my shoulders in an attempt to comfort me. The only thing I noticed was that she was much more boney and hard than my mother. I ran into the bathroom and threw up.

For the next hour or so, I sat outside the emergency room where my mother lay dead and waited for the doctors to finish dressing a few bruises on my father's face and legs. Another couple, who had offered to drive my parents home after my mother had urged my fatigued sister to leave the party early, were being treated for injuries. But my mother was the only one of the four who had died. She had been thrown from the backseat of the car, out the passenger door, and onto the hard asphalt road. When the police arrived at the scene, they had found my father cradling my mother's head in his lap, desperately trying to stop the blood flowing from her mouth. It had been no use.

At this point, no one knew where my sister and my brother-in-law were. I tried calling their apartment every few minutes, but I got no answer. As I sat in total confusion on a metal bench in the hallway, the coroner arrived. He had been awakened and he seemed quite irritated. He urged me to identify the body of my mother, who had died instantly from punctured lungs, a skull concussion, two broken legs, and massive internal injuries. I told him I couldn't bear to see her alone.

"But I don't have much time," the coroner told me impatiently. "I have to get back home."

I shuddered, and for some reason remembered the time I had imposed my deadline on the grieving mother of the Vietnam casualty. I tried calling my sister again. Finally, after about ten rings, she answered in a sleepy voice. My God, I thought, how could she be sleeping at a time like this?

"Where have you been?" I shouted with the anxiety of a mother scolding a lost child.

"What are you talking about?" Mary answered. "The air-conditioner was on and it muffled the phone. Why, what's wrong?"

I told her that Mommy and Daddy had been in a car accident. I almost could hear her head snap up from the pillow.

"Are they all right?" my sister asked with fear in her voice.

"Just get here as fast as you can," I said, not wanting to break the news over the phone.

As I waited for Mary to arrive, I thought back to the day my mother had rushed into the emergency room after my car accident. I wished I had brought along some smelling salts. Just as I felt I was going to faint, the coroner walked up and urged me once again to identify my mother's broken body. I finally agreed. I later wished I hadn't.

When I walked into the tiny room where my mother's body lay, I almost did not recognize her. Her face was swollen to twice its normal size from the impact of the collision. Her mouth was caked with blood. Her cheeks already were turning blue. The coroner told me that I could kiss her if I wanted. I didn't want to. I wanted to remember my mother as soft and warm and wonderfully alive. I ran out of the room. But I could not cry.

Later that day, I sat down and spilled out my anguish in a weekly column I then was writing for the *Daily Times*. I was so hurt and agonized that I could not use the pronoun "I." Instead, I chose to write with the more impersonal "you." The column appeared in print the following Friday, the day of my mother's funeral.

> You don't know what it is to meet the cold, dark whiteness of a hospital emergency room until you walk in one night, pleading in your heart for the impossible and finding the inevitable. "Your mother didn't make it," the nurse tells you.
>
> You can become very cold and callous about accidents and obituaries until you are in the center of this horrible, bloody business of death. Then you lose control and you stand stunned and you want terribly to wake up from this unspeakable nightmare.
>
> But you can't wake up no matter how hard you try and white uniforms and mumbled concern and antiseptic smells blur in your mind. It can't be true that your mother is dead and you pray desperately

the whole thing is some ghastly joke and everything will be just fine.

But she is dead and nothing will be just fine, ever again. It is all over between you and her, those twenty years of tears and laughter, heartache and joy.

This is your mother under that starched hospital sheet, covered up forever from the harsh glance of life. It is the woman who gave you your life.

The eyes that are closed now were the ones that stayed open each evening watching Huntley and Brinkley, reading the newspaper from the want ads to the marriage licenses, carefully examining each stitch of her embroidery. They are the eyes, the blue beautiful eyes, that cried so piercingly when her own mother died.

This is the mouth that talked with an Irish brogue and kept all your secrets inside and told you once that you had always been a joy to her. It is the same mouth that kissed you the day before this nightmare and thanked you for putting up her hair for the last time.

These are the hands that taught you how to write your name and tie your shoelaces and dress yourself. They are the hands with the thin silver wedding band, worn down after twenty-five years of marriage.

And these are the feet that sometimes walked to your grammar school to take you out for a hot turkey lunch, something none of the other kids did. They are the feet that stood so many times by your sickbed and waited until you came back from surgery.

These are the arms that encircled you when you cried over a dead turtle or a bruised knee or the horrible tragedy of a broken romance. They are the arms that washed and ironed your clothing and did a million things that you never bothered to thank her for.

And here are the shoulders where you rested during your inconsolable sorrows when she told you that time would heal all wounds and joy would come again. It is hard to believe that now.

It is hard to believe that these are the knees that cradled you as a child and gave you the safest haven in the world. Her lap was the place where she taught you and your sister how to read by going through the comics every night and explaining all the words.

This is the woman who spent her life loving and living for her husband, her two daughters, her sisters and her friends. She is the one who occasionally lost her temper and never held a grudge or said an unkind word about anybody.

She is the mother who helped you and your sister through every sorrow and laughed with you through every joy. Here is the woman who succeeded in loving her two children as individuals and showing favoritism to neither one.

And now, in this cold darkness of a hospital emergency room, there is no one to console you anymore. There are only blinding lights and starched uniforms and antiseptic smells.

Your mother does not belong in a place like this, but she is bruised and broken and gone forever. You cry because you were not there to console her. And you never had a chance to thank her or to say good-bye.

I also wrote my mother's obituary that day, being very careful to mention all of her twelve surviving brothers and sisters. When it came to revealing her age, however, I did something regarded as totally unethical for a reporter: I lied. My mother had lopped anywhere from five to fifteen years off of her age for most of her life and I didn't want to reveal her secret now.

Partly because she was my mother and partly because Sunday is traditionally a slow news day, my mother's death appeared the Monday after the accident on page one of the *Daily Times*. The only other major story in that issue was an advance on the opening of the Republican National Convention; the headline read NIXON PUSHES HARD FOR FIRST BALLOT WIN. I felt that it was a shame that my mother never had a chance to see the first and only time her name ever appeared in the newspaper. But I knew that she would have appreciated the fact that the headline on her obituary was larger than the headline on the news story about Nixon.

Because of all the publicity, I began receiving hundreds of sympathy cards and letters from people I had never met. One woman said she hung my column near her telephone so that she wouldn't forget to call her own elderly mother every day. A man wrote that his son had cried his eyes out when he read about my mother's death. Another reader told me I had a standing invitation to eat dinner at her home every Mother's Day.

To say the least, I was profoundly touched by all of the mail. A few days after the funeral, I received a telegram from New York. I couldn't imagine who had read the *Daily Times* there. Curious, I opened it before any of the regular mail.

It was the Newspaper Fund, sponsors of the contest my mother had urged me to enter. I had won the top prize and another five hundred dollars. For the first time since my mother's death, I began to cry, with shaking, breathless sobs. I knew now that winning never would be quite the same again.

I had lost my biggest fan.

2--Disasters

Monroe Monseur had borrowed an aluminum outboard boat for the weekend and had invited a photographer and me along for the ride. It was not exactly a pleasure outing; Monseur, a wig manufacturer from Wilkes-Barre, Pennsylvania, was navigating through five feet of floodwaters in an effort to reach his heavily damaged hairpiece shop.

"Well, I guess I've lost everything," Monseur said as several wigs floated by the outboard motor as we approached his waterlogged store.

It was Sunday, June 25, 1972, the day after Tropical Storm Agnes had destroyed almost 100,000 homes in upstate Pennsylvania during one of the worst natural disasters in United States history. The Philadelphia *Inquirer*, where I was now working, had sent photographer Bill Steinmetz and me to Wilkes-Barre, a small town that was reported to be the scene of the heaviest flooding. It was not as bad as we had expected. It was a lot worse.

More than twenty-four hours after the city's dam had

burst, most of the town's 50,000 homes still were underwater. The only thing visible from the boat were the roofs of houses, the tops of street signs, the upper leaves of massive oak trees. In one hilly area of town, a group of residents stood on their tiptoes in an attempt to catch sight of their homes. Few succeeded; it would be another full day before the waters began to recede.

But I couldn't wait for nature to take its course. The *Inquirer* editors wanted some closeup pictures and on-the-scene interviews for Monday's paper. Luckily, Monseur had happened along and offered us a ride in his boat. And although he had just lost his home, his office, and his entire inventory in the flood, he refused to take a cent for his trouble.

"We all have to help one another out at a time like this," he said.

Like most people, I had never witnessed a major disaster before. As Bill and I were making the four-hour ride that morning from Philadelphia, I realized that the only flood I had ever seen was in the basement of a childhood friend, her mother's washing machine had overflowed, and I, feeling like a six-year-old heroine, had helped bale out the cellar with buckets. I envisioned a similar scene in Wilkes-Barre, but with larger buckets.

Was I ever wrong! As we rode through the residential section of the city, I was horrified by the extent of the damage. Entire rows of houses had been knocked from their foundations by the force of the water and were now leaning against one another like fallen dominoes. Electrical wiring was hanging like burned spaghetti from ceiling after ceiling. Wall-to-wall carpeting looked like nothing more than mounds of mud.

Yet, with the strength of spirit often noticed during great human tragedy, the people of Wilkes-Barre were reacting to the flood with incredible good humor. Mother Nature had become the leveler not only of the buildings but also of the people; rich and poor were literally in the same boat.

In one neighborhood, a prominent lawyer was helping an automobile mechanic pull his car out of the mud. The maître d' at a local restaurant was dishing out potato salad at a Red Cross emergency shelter. Most doctors in town were giving free typhoid shots.

"I'm definitely going to start over again," Monseur said as he maneuvered the boat around some floating debris. "Everyone will chip in and help. People are really together in this thing."

Because it was getting late and deadline was only five hours away, we asked Monseur if he could take us back to our car. The original plan was to drive back to Philadelphia and get our stories and pictures in for the second edition about 9 P.M. We called the city desk to tell them what we had seen.

"Sounds like you should stay," an editor said. "It'll be a great story when the water goes down and the people see their homes for the first time."

Because the flood had shut down the local newspaper, Bill figured the fastest way to get his film to Philadelphia would be to drive twenty-five miles to Hazleton and put it on a Greyhound bus. A copyboy would pick it up on the other end and take it to the city room. The plan suited me just fine because it would give me time to write my story en route and dictate it over the phone from Hazleton. Ordinarily on fast-breaking out-of-town stories, a reporter can call in the facts to a rewrite person, who then actually composes the article. But, whenever possible, I preferred to eliminate the middle person and write the finished piece myself.

Later that evening, Bill and I went to Pocono Downs Racetrack, where the Red Cross had set up an emergency shelter for about three thousand homeless flood victims. The scene was a photographer's dream: thousands of cots stretched out on the grandstand bleachers; displaced residents lined up at the Exacta window getting typhoid shots; airplanes landing on the track with much-needed food and clothing.

By this time, it was close to 10 P.M. and I suddenly realized I hadn't eaten anything all day. I also realized that I had no change of clothing for the following morning, since I hadn't expected to stay in Wilkes-Barre overnight. The clothes I was wearing, like the entire city, were covered with mud.

"Ah, and to think most people think reporters lead glamorous lives." I laughed as I combed some mud out of my hair.

One of the volunteer aides standing nearby heard my lament and told me to take some of the clothing arranged in neat piles all over the basement of the racetrack. Feeling a little guilty, I went over to take a look at the pile marked SIZE TEN. I selected the ugliest jacket and pants I could find because I didn't want to take good clothing from people who really needed it. I rushed off to a makeshift dressing room to put on my new duds. I emerged a few minutes later wearing my newly acquired red-plaid hunter's jacket and baggy green army pants.

"Wow, I look just like a cover girl," I mused. "For *Field and Stream*."

The following morning, the floodwaters finally began to go down. There were rumors that out-of-towners already had begun looting stores, so businessmen were the first people permitted back into town. The scene was full of more bizarre images: a nude mannequin washed up on the steps of a Catholic church; diamond rings floating in a puddle outside a jewelry store; bathtubs in a plumbing supply store prefilled with floodwater.

That afternoon I met a man who had lost both his home and his auto dealership in the disaster. Earlier in the day he had taken one look at his car showroom and returned to a hotel on the outskirts of town, where most of the press, including me, also were staying. It didn't take much perception to figure out how the man was handling his sorrows; two empty quarts of Scotch were sitting on the bureau of his room. His wife was wringing her hands in anguish.

"We're both eating everything in sight and drinking everything that flows," the man told me. "Why not? Everything else we own is all wet."

Later that night, hundreds of National Guardsmen were called into town to protect what little was left of residents' property. The rumors of looting were all true; some opportunists had actually rented boats a hundred miles away in order to steal from unoccupied homes and businesses. Because the electricity had not yet been restored, several power companies had set up emergency floodlights to illuminate the streets. The lighting, plus the heavily armed troops, provided an eerie sight.

But not nearly so eerie as the sight I saw the next day.

As Bill and I were eating breakfast in the motel coffee shop, we overheard someone talking about a cemetery in Forty Fort, Pennsylvania, about ten miles outside of Wilkes-Barre.

"Bodies washed up . . . one corpse found hanging in a tree after the water went down . . . a casket came floating down the street. . . ."

Bill and I looked at each other in amazement. He threw

down his napkin and began running back to his room for his camera.

"Hey, what about my eggs?" I yelled, looking longingly at the omelet-plate special that had just arrived on my place mat.

"Take it with you," Bill yelled back.

"Right," I said, taking solace in the fact that I'd probably arrive back in Philadelphia five pounds lighter if this kept up.

As we approached the cemetery, I could see from a distance that the metal fence surrounding the graveyard had been bent and twisted by the force of the water. The sign announcing FORTY FORT BURIAL GROUNDS was half buried in the ground itself. Several trees were completely uprooted, their gnarled roots now fully exposed in the sunlight.

Bill's car screeched to a halt. I was beginning to feel very uneasy about tramping through a cemetery without permission. I also felt uneasy about adding to the desecration of the flood waters. But, mostly, I felt uneasy about the prospect of seeing a bunch of decaying bodies lying all over the place.

"Oh, come on," Bill said as I expressed my intention to go back to the car.

Pushing aside my personal feelings, I had to admit that the devastated cemetery might be a good story. So I plunged forward. I tiptoed up to the gate and slowly entered. As I was walking toward the main section of the cemetery, my right foot suddenly sank into a pile of mud. Thinking I had fallen into a grave, I let out a frightened yelp. I wanted to scream bloody murder.

"Come on, come on," Bill said.

When we got to the burial area, the upheaval was every bit as appalling as we had heard: tombstones were lying in pieces, caskets were standing upright against tree trunks, vacant holes were gaping at us from the hillside.

Trying hard to act casual, I gazed into one of the recently vacated graves. A skull gazed back at me.

"I think I'm going to be sick," I said.

After covering Tropical Storm Agnes' effects in Wilkes-Barre and other upstate Pennsylvania towns, I thought I had seen everything as far as natural disasters were concerned. Then, two years later, I was dispatched to Brandenburg, Kentucky, which had been heavily damaged by an unexpected tornado. I soon learned that I hadn't seen anything yet.

On Wednesday afternoon, April 3, 1974, Associated Press and United Press International, which send teletype stories to newspapers around the world, were reporting that the tornado had killed more than 330 persons as it whipped its destructive path through ten states in the eastern half of the country. The worst-hit states were Kentucky and Indiana. By late Wednesday night, AP and UPI said that the death toll in Brandenburg, Kentucky, a town of only 1,700 people already had hit forty. The *Inquirer* decided to call me at home and send me to interview the survivors.

"We've got pictures from the wire, so we don't need a photographer," an editor said. "But you get there as fast as you can."

"As fast as I can" turned out to be pretty slow. Contrary to popular misconceptions, newspaper reporters rarely enjoy the luxury of prearranged plane tickets, car rentals, or hotel accommodations. Nine times out of ten, they have to work out all the travel details themselves.

I immediately picked up the phone and called my favorite airline to see if they had a late-night flight to Louisville. Nothing. I called my second-favorite airline.

The same thing—nothing. I called a third airline, which I had never heard of before. They didn't have a flight either. Back to the first airline.

"The best I can do is fly you out of Philadelphia tomorrow at eight-fifteen A.M. to Washington, D.C., and then transfer you to a flight to Louisville at ten-fifteen," the reservationist said. "That should get you in Kentucky by noon."

It didn't. Because of air-traffic delays, my plane from Washington to Louisville was an hour late taking off. I spent sixty nervous minutes at Dulles Airport reading the New York *Times* account of the Brandenburg disaster and wondering how their reporter had gotten there so soon. By the time I landed in Kentucky, it was after 1 P.M. It had taken me five hours to make a flight that should have taken two.

"Please, get me a car quick," I said, running over to the car-rental counter. "I'm in a big hurry."

"Well, lady, you've come to the wrong place," the rental agent said. "There have been all kinds of government people coming in here because of the tornado. We don't have a single car left."

"Well, could you give me the first one that comes in?" I asked in desperation.

"Sure, sure," the man said. "I'll let you know when I have anything."

A car was finally returned at 2 P.M. I had exactly four hours to drive fifty miles to Brandenburg, interview a dozen or so people, write the story, and call it into the *Inquirer.* It was going to be tight.

It was even tighter than I had expected. When I finally got a mile outside Brandenburg, I found that the entire town had been cordoned off for a mile all around. The state police zealously were making sure that no unauthorized vehicles got past the barriers. Unhappily, I was driving an unauthorized vehicle.

"Sorry, lady, you can't go in there," a trooper told me as I tried to drive around a road block.

"But I have to," I said, identifying myself as a reporter for the Philadelphia *Inquirer*.

"No reporters are allowed," he replied.

I knew this was not true because I had just read the article in the New York *Times*. The statement infuriated me. And I told the trooper so.

"It's not fair that you let other reporters in and then try to keep me out," I spluttered. "I have to get in there for my job."

"Well, okay, you can go in but not your car," he said.

"Okay, I'll park it right over there," I said, pointing to the shoulder of the road.

"Oh, no, you can't park on this road," the trooper said. "You'll have to go somewhere else."

I was obviously getting nowhere with this man. It was time to make a quick decision. Should I drive out of town, and risk losing not only precious minutes but also the entire story? Or should I just disregard the trooper, leave my car on the shoulder, and start walking?

I left the car and started walking.

"Look, I know you're trying to do your job, but so am I," I said as the trooper yelled obscenities at me. "So tow the car away if you have to."

Outwardly, I wanted to give the trooper the impression that the car was rented anyway, so what did I care? Inwardly, I was hoping that the police would be too busy coping with the tornado victims to bother towing the car. At any rate, like Scarlett O'Hara, I would deal with the problem later. It was after 3 P.M., less than three hours to go until deadline.

As I was half jogging, half limping down the road leading to the main section of town, a pickup truck pulled up alongside of me.

"Hey, want a ride?" asked the driver, a young man wearing denim overalls.

For some reason I had a fleeting image of my mother warning me as a child never to accept rides with strangers, especially if they offered me candy. I didn't see any candy.

"Sure, I'd love a ride," I said. "Thanks a lot."

As it turned out, the driver was a volunteer fireman from a neighboring town who had come to Brandenburg to see if he could help. I don't know if he got a chance to help any residents, but he certainly helped me. He spent the next two hours chauffeuring me from house to house.

When we got to the center of town, I was once again astounded by the wrath and force of Mother Nature. In many sections of Brandenburg, the twister had sucked up entire houses, cars, and worst of all, human beings, and then dropped them miles away.

The pickup-truck driver stopped by a curb where a young man was sifting through some rubble that used to be the roof of his grandparents' home. His grandfather had been found dead inside the house; his grandmother had been killed when the tornado swirled her into the air and then dumped her two miles away. She was found buried beneath three cars.

"I remember my grandmother carrying this," the young man said, picking up a pocketbook lying on the sidewalk. "I just can't believe anything like this could happen to them."

Neither could I. At times like this, I never could comprehend the injustices of the world: why certain people seem to be chosen to bear almost unbearable sorrows. There never is any answer. The young man who had lost his grandparents seemed to be bearing up as well as could be expected. Once again, I was torn between my roles as a reporter and as a human being. On the one hand, I wanted to make sure I had the correct spellings of the names of the tornado victims; on the other, I didn't want to burden the bereaved grandson with my journalistic problems. As sometimes happens with victims of great tragedies, however, the man seemed almost eager to talk. He spelled his grandparents' names before I even asked.

At the end of our conversation, I reached out my arm and put it around the saddened man. I told him I was terribly sorry. He held my hand for several minutes before letting go.

A few blocks away, I met a man whose wife and newborn baby had been swept away in the tornado. He had been at work when it happened. Neighbors told me the man blamed himself for not being at home to protect his family. Indeed, when I saw him, the grief-stricken husband was walking around with a dazed expression on his face. He said he was not able to talk about it. I nodded sympathetically and slipped away. I didn't feel much like playing investigative reporter.

By the time I had talked to a few more tornado victims and rescue workers, it was close to 5 P.M. I figured that I better get back to my car, scribble down some notes, and beat it to the nearest telephone. If my car still was there, that is.

Miraculously, it was. I thanked my chauffeur for the ride and drove to the nearest diner. I ran in and asked to use their phone.

"You've got to be kidding," a waitress said. "There

aren't any phones working for twenty-five miles around."

Moments earlier, I would not have believed that anything else could go wrong. But it had. This truly qualified as "one of those days." I jumped back in the car and started driving down the highway, holding on to the steering wheel with my left hand and scribbling notes with the right.

By the time I reached a working telephone, it was 6 P.M., deadline for the first edition. I had organized the facts of my story on paper and was ready to dictate.

"Hello, hello," I said to one of the editors on the national desk. "I got the story."

"Great, great," he said. "Hold on and I'll give you to another reporter."

I heard a click. And then another click. And then the phone went dead.

"Operator, operator," I yelled into the phone.

But there was no answer.

My feelings of frustration were overwhelming. Despite all the odds against me that day, I had managed to get the story. But now I couldn't get it to the paper. I angrily slammed the receiver down and kicked the wall of the phone booth.

I got back into the rental car and began cruising down the highway, stopping at every roadside phone. None of them worked. I knew I already had missed the first edition, but I wanted at least to get the story in for the final.

By the time I got to a phone that worked, it was 8 P.M. I tried to imagine what the editors were thinking. That I had had a heart attack? That I had been kidnapped? Or, worst of all, that I didn't really get the story?

But they were more imaginative than that.

"Oh, God, thank heaven you're safe," the night editor said when I finally got through. "We thought the tornado had blown the phone booth away."

That was a possibility I hadn't even considered. I burst out laughing. It was the first time I had laughed all day.

"Wow, what a great first-person story that would have been," I said.

3 -- The Office

Nancy Hayfield, a fellow reporter at the *Daily Times*, sauntered over to my desk and said that she had a "big secret" to tell me. We immediately rushed into the ladies' room, which was the only place away from the crowded newsroom to hold a private conversation.

"I'm going to get married and have a big wedding and invite everyone from the paper," Nancy confided. "And I'd like to know if you would like to be a bridesmaid."

Would I ever! Although I had been a reporter for several months at this point, I still didn't feel as if I truly belonged to the unique social circle of the newsroom. Because I was only eighteen, I felt very awkward and shy around most of my co-workers. Apart from Nancy, they were, after all, old men and old women in their late twenties and early thirties. But, despite the age difference, I wanted desperately to be considered one of the gang. And I saw the wedding as my big chance. It would be my first social contact with my co-workers outside the office.

On the Saturday of the wedding I dressed very carefully in order to appear older and more sophisticated than I really was. I dabbed on some extra blusher. I applied a touch of eyeliner. I doused myself in exotic Japanese perfume.

"You look just beautiful," said my mother, who always said that.

"Do I really?" I asked, forcing her to say it again.

At any rate, the wedding unquestionably was beautiful. The church was bedecked with magnificent flowers. The foyer was dramatized by an archway made from the swords of a military honor guard. The guests were dressed in their finest fancy clothes.

The only flaw as far as I was concerned was that I had forgotten to eat breakfast. And as Nancy and her bridegroom exchanged their final vows, my stomach punctuated their promises with some embarrassingly loud growls. I was dying of hunger and thirst.

When we got to the reception at a lovely waterfront restaurant near Philadelphia International Airport, almost everyone headed straight for the punch bowl, which was dispensing something that looked and tasted like Kool-Aid. I didn't care what it was as long as it was ice cold and plentiful and refreshing. It was. I drank six glasses.

By the time dinner was ready to be served, I realized that something was terribly wrong. My head was spinning. My stomach was churning. My knees were wobbling. In other words, I was dead drunk.

"Will everyone please be seated," announced the master of ceremonies over the loudspeaker. "We now are ready for the grand march."

In my foggy condition I vaguely recalled that the plan was for each couple in the bridal party to walk up to the dais separately after being introduced at the entranceway to the dining room. I wasn't sure I was going to make it.

"Hold on," said the military cadet who was my partner in the wedding.

And that's what I did. By the time our names were called, it was all I could do to hang tightly on to my partner's arm as he half carried me to the main dais. I tried to pull myself together as we passed two tables occupied by my bosses at the *Daily Times*, but I had little success. Of course, by this time I didn't much care. I giddily congratulated myself on my savoir faire when I finally reached the bridal table. Then one of the cadets pulled out my chair and I prepared to sit down. I missed. I fell flat on the floor.

By this point I was totally oblivious to my own pain, much less the bride's. I scrambled up to participate in the best man's toast. But I couldn't seem to direct the glass to my mouth and I spilled wine all over the floor. Feeling somewhat abashed, I leaned down to wipe up the puddle. I pulled the tablecloth along with me and the silverware came thumping down on my head.

"I think I better be excused," I said as someone helped me to the ladies' room.

Even in my inebriated state, I was suddenly clutched with pangs of conscience. My God, I thought, here I am ruining Nancy's wedding by making such a spectacle of myself. There clearly was only one sensible thing to do: I would lie down under the sink in the ladies' room and no one would notice me.

"I think people are going to notice you," another bridesmaid said when she walked in and found me trying to curl myself unobtrusively around the plumbing pipes.

The next few minutes were a blur. Everyone was out of focus: the waiter who peeped his head in the door and called for help; the manager who came rushing in with oxygen; the four cadets who marched in and, with drill-team precision, hoisted me onto their shoulders and carried me out over the heads of the surprised guests.

The last thing I remember were the faces of some of the *Daily Times* reporters and editors whom I had wanted so much to impress. And then everything went black.

The following Monday, having suffered through the most excruciating headache of my life, I was terribly embarrassed about the entire incident. I never wanted to go back to the city room again. I was certain I had ruined my chances not only of becoming "one of the guys" but also of ever becoming a reporter.

When I got to the doorway of the newsroom that morning, I held my breath in anticipation. I secretly was hoping upon hope that the reporters and editors had forgotten about my bizarre behavior. They hadn't.

As I walked into the room, every reporter turned and stared. One reached out his arm and pointed directly at me. If there had been any plumbing pipes in sight, I would have crawled under them again.

"Begley, that was the funniest thing I ever saw," chortled one reporter who had never even acknowledged my presence before. "You're okay."

And then the rest of the reporters stood up and cheered. I couldn't believe it. At long last, I was IN.

Years later, when I told a friend about this incident, she couldn't believe the casual reaction not only of my fellow reporters but also of my editors. She had worked once in a business office where everything was carefully regulated, right down to office location and decor: top executives occupied offices with wall-to-wall carpeting; junior executives occupied offices with area rugs; and lowly secretaries occupied cubicles in the hallway with no rugs at all. Everyone, at all times, was expected to dress properly, speak properly, and behave properly. My friend said I probably would have been fired for my conduct at Nancy's wedding. All of which accounts for the fact that I never have had any desire to work in an ordinary office atmosphere.

By and large, newspapers seem far more tolerant of the peculiarities and quirks of their employees than most employers, which is lucky for me because I am loaded with peculiarities and quirks. Most editors and reporters are so single-minded about putting the paper out on time that they seem to have little interest in imposing additional strictures on themselves. Daily deadline is enough stricture for anyone. As a result, newspaper city rooms seem to show a total lack of concern about matters of great concern in ordinary businesses: dress and decor, for example.

After graduating from Temple University in January 1970, I left the *Daily Times*, which had a circulation at that time of about 50,000, to work at the *Courier-Post* in Camden, N. J., which had a circulation of about 120,000. When I arrived for my first day at the *Courier*, I noticed immediately that most of the female reporters were wearing demure dresses and dressy, low-heeled shoes. I was wearing a miniskirt and boots.

A few months later one of my bosses mentioned that my attire, which sometimes included blue jeans, was certainly unorthodox but didn't seem to interfere with my work. My beat at the time was leftist politics and urban affairs.

"How could blue jeans interfere with my work?" I asked. "I look well dressed compared to most of the people I'm dealing with."

Not long after I joined the *Inquirer* in April 1971, I began to wear blue jeans routinely, no matter whom I was going to interview. It never once affected my getting the story. On the contrary, I often found that conservative businessmen and politicians were often less inhibited with me than with my more conservatively dressed peers. I sometimes suspected that some of my sources never expected to see their statements appear on page one of a major metropolitan newspaper.

"I thought you were some teenybopper," one interviewee once told me. "I couldn't believe it when I saw the story in print."

Of course, not everyone agrees with me about dressing casually as a news reporter. My friend Jan Schaffer, who started working at the *Inquirer* the year after I did, dressed every day like a fashion model right out of *Women's Wear Daily*. She told me that she feared professional sources would be turned off by unprofessional attire. Perhaps she's right.

One day while I was working at the *Inquirer* a friend came up to the city room to meet me for lunch. She never had been in a newspaper office before and she couldn't believe her eyes: trash cans were filled to overflowing; desks were piled high with month-old newspapers; filing cabinets were topped with mounds of magazines and books. What's more, most of the desks were squashed together in the middle of the room. There were only a few glass enclosures, but even these often were occupied by several persons.

"But doesn't anyone have an office?" she asked in amazement. "I mean, how do you tell who's boss?"

"You don't," I said with a grin. "That's the beauty of it."

Whatever the reasons, I am totally convinced that newspaper people are different from any other professional group. Perhaps because they are trained to remain objective in reporting stories, they rarely get emotionally involved in insignificant and irrelevant office traditions like nameplates and pen sets. But when a particular situation truly concerns them, they make up for it with more emotion than ordinarily seen on a television soap opera.

One time after my vacation at the *Daily Times*, for instance, I returned to a nearly empty newsroom: most of my co-workers had walked off the job in a dispute over the firing of a single staffer. At the *Courier-Post*, one reporter was so emotionally overwrought about company policies that he cut off his hair in protest and left it on the publisher's desk. At the *Inquirer*, one writer had such a legendary quick temper that people barely noticed every time he got up from his chair and began flailing his arms in anger, which was often.

But the emotional involvement wasn't always negative. In 1975, when I had been working at the *Inquirer* for four years, several editors became involved in a subject near and dear to my heart: me. I became very ill, and Max King, then regional editor and my boss, did everything but go into a laboratory and come up with a cure.

I first noticed that something was wrong with my legs in March 1975, while I was working on a story about traveling saleswomen. To get background on what the job was like, I accompanied a cosmetics saleswoman on her rounds to various department stores and drugstores. We made about twenty stops one day, but walked only a few blocks at any given time. Yet, when I got home later, I was utterly exhausted. And my legs ached as they had never ached before.

By April I was in real pain almost constantly. I remember one assignment that month where I was sent to interview a woman whose seven-year-old daughter had been shot for no apparent reason by a passing motorist. As she told me about how she had scooped her bleeding child into her arms, my eyes brimmed with tears. I'm not sure whether they were caused by the mother's sad tale or the throbbing pain in my ankles and feet.

That night I drove to Wilmington, Delaware, where my father now lives. I was drinking a cup of tea on his sofa when he put on his eyeglasses and peered closely at my legs. They had been swollen for about a week, but I had refused to admit it to anyone, including myself.

"Kathleen, me dear," my father said in the Irish brogue he never lost in the forty years he's lived in the United States, "your legs shouldn't be swollen like that. You must go to the doctor."

I pretended to my father that I wasn't worried. But on Friday, two days later, I could no longer pretend. When I woke up that morning, my ankles and knees were so swollen and stiffened that I barely could walk.

"Max, I won't be in today," I said when I called the city room. "I have to go to the doctor and find out what's wrong with me."

A few hours later I wished I hadn't. The doctor, who had been recommended by my gynecologist, did not mince words about my condition. He took one look at my legs and said he was fairly positive about the diagnosis.

"I'm afraid it's rheumatoid arthritis," he said, shaking his head. "You have all of the symptoms."

Rheumatoid arthritis. To me, the words stung like the word "cancer." Only recently I had learned that one of my high-school classmates had developed the same disease. And at twenty-eight she was confined to a wheelchair and was expected never to walk again. I began shaking.

"Look, we'll have some tests done," the doctor said. "But I wouldn't to be too hopeful."

Believe me, I wasn't. After the doctor left the examination room, I sat still for a few moments before dressing, to sort out my feelings. I just couldn't believe the bad timing of my illness.

Just a few months earlier, I had met a wonderful man named Wiley Brooks, and he and I were making long-range plans for a beautiful life together. For the first time since my mother's death, my father seemed content and free from worry. Besides that, my career had progressed to the point where I was frequently traveling all over the country on assignment. Why did this have to happen to me now?

When I stepped out to the doctor's waiting room, Wiley was waiting to hear the diagnosis. I couldn't bear to tell him. I fell limply into his arms. He held me tight.

"Arthritis?" he asked softly.

"Yes." I nodded.

"Don't you worry," he comforted me. "Everything will be all right."

Although the doctor had advised me to check into the hospital immediately for testing, I persuaded him to let me give blood samples in the out-patient laboratory. Afterwards, Wiley and I drove immediately to the *Inquirer*. I wanted to explain the situation to Max. And I also wanted to find out everything I could about rheumatoid arthritis.

All through my career I had frequently used the clippings and books in newspaper offices to look up information needed by me or my friends: reading skills statistics for a former teacher; information on women's liberation for a feminist acquaintance; Irish history for myself. I always had considered use of a newspaper library as a marvelous fringe benefit, but never so much as now.

I searched through the office for every piece of information I could get my hands on: stories on arthritis that had appeared in past issues of the *Inquirer*; excerpts from medical books; manila folders of magazine stories clipped by Donald Drake, the paper's prize-winning medical writer. All of the materials plunged me into deeper despair. Almost every article began in the same way: "Rheumatoid arthritis is one of the most painful and crippling forms of arthritis. There is no known cure."

Depressed, I went home and crawled wearily into bed. The doctor had told me that I would have to go into the hospital on Monday if there was no improvement over the weekend from the medication he had prescribed to ease the pain.

On Saturday my symptoms were worse. My ankles and knees were still swollen and now my hands were too. When I went into the bathroom to brush my teeth, my fingers were so stiff that I couldn't get the cap off the toothpaste tube. I felt totally useless.

The next morning began one of the worst days in my life. When I tried to get up to answer the telephone, I couldn't walk. My feet were curled up with stiffness and pain. I fell on the floor. Wiley picked me up and tried to console me. But I was inconsolable. I couldn't bear the thought of having to be carried everywhere, including the bathroom.

All through the weekend the doctor called several times a day. So did Max. They both asked the same questions: Had the swelling gone down? Was I still in pain? Was the stiffness getting worse? Although I hadn't noticed any improvement, I told the doctor that I would like to stay at home for a few more days. I had a terrible fear that if I went into the hospital, I might never come out.

On Monday I insisted that Wiley go to work. He insisted that he stay with me. I won—but only because I made an awful scene. Before leaving, Wiley thoughtfully gathered everything I might need and put it within my reach: a bedpan, books, telephone, magazines, nail polish. The bed was so crowded that there hardly was room for me.

After Wiley was gone, I got down to some serious business: feeling sorry for myself. My career obviously was over: I couldn't stand, I couldn't walk, I couldn't even hold a pencil. I was enraged one moment, despondent the next.

Then Max called.

"We found an arthritis specialist," Max said. "Here's his number; give him a call."

I did. But the nurse said the doctor wouldn't be able to see me for about two months. I cringed. I figured I'd be completely crippled by then. I told her to forget it.

Max called back and told me that several people in the office were working on my case. Gene Roberts, the executive editor, had contacted some medical experts he had worked with at the New York *Times*. Donald Drake was researching medical journals to learn about any possible breakthroughs in the treatment of arthritis. Even Max's father, a New England physician I had never met, was checking possible sources of help. I was deeply moved by all the concern.

"How did you make out with the doctor I told you about?" Max asked. "When is your appointment?"

When I told him about the long delay, Max said he would look into the problem. To this day I don't know what he did, but it certainly got results. Ten minutes later, the nurse called back to say the doctor would see me at the end of the week. I always have suspected that the medical office suddenly was deluged with calls from every editor at the *Inquirer*. But Max, in his own modest way, never said.

During the next few days the swelling in my hands, legs, and feet started to go down. The morning stiffness in my joints also began to disappear. By the day of my appointment, I almost felt normal.

When he saw me, the specialist said I had no outward signs of arthritis. But he added that symptoms sometimes disappear temporarily at the outset of the disease. He sent me to the laboratory for another round of blood tests. The results of my first tests had just been returned from the pathologist. Oddly enough, they had been negative.

I returned to the specialist a few days later, expecting to hear the worst. But the second tests also had been negative. Although the stiffness and swelling had not reappeared, the doctor wanted to be sure. So he decided to send me for my third set of blood tests. Although I was starting to feel like a pincushion, I wanted to find out for certain exactly what was wrong. But I never did.

The following week the doctor said the third series of tests also showed no biological evidence of arthritis. Yet he had no explanation of why I had experienced such painful swelling and stiffness. I didn't know whether to laugh or cry; it was as if I had had a death warrant lifted from my head, but I would never know who had framed me in the crime. But at least I had a reprieve.

For the next year I awoke every morning with a slight dread that my feet and ankles would be swollen and stiffened again. They never were. My anxieties began to go away.

Since then, I have often thought about all the wonderful moral support I have received from my newspaper co-workers. When my mother died, Helen Hunt, one of the reporters at the *Daily Times,* arrived at my home carrying a week's worth of home-cooked meals. When my father was very sick, Carolyn Zachary, an editor at the *Courier-Post,* forced me to leave early several afternoons so I could make it on time to the hospital. And when I myself became so ill, Max showed so much conern that I often have thought that I should have paid him instead of the doctors.

A lot of people have an image of journalists as skeptical, hard, bitter and cynical. Who says?

4--National News

The taxi whizzed past the White House, sped down Connecticut Avenue, and screeched to a halt outside the Mayflower Hotel. As soon as the cab stopped, a bellhop opened the door and took out our bags.

"Ah, yes, Miss Begley, welcome to the Mayflower," he said, cleverly learning my name by glancing at the name tag on my suitcase. "Watch your step getting out of the cab."

I was thrilled.

It was June 1967, and I was covering my first out-of-town story: the fortieth annual National Spelling Bee sponsored by Scripps-Howard Newspapers. Like many newspapers around the nation, the *Daily Times* had sent a local winner on an all-expense-paid trip to the finals in Washington, D.C. And I was assigned to report on the local youth's spelling progress. To be sure, the assignment wasn't exactly like covering the White House, but I wasn't complaining. After all, I was only nineteen years old, and I had $300 in expense money, and I was going to stay at a sumptuous Washington hotel. I felt golden.

Before boarding the train that morning in Chester, the spelling champion, Steve Markowski, and his mother, Anne, and I had posed for all kinds of pictures for the *Daily Times* photographer. All during the two-hour ride to Washington, we sat giggling over the other passengers trying to figure out just who we were. I alternated pretending to be Elizabeth Taylor and Ali McGraw.

By the time we arrived, the Mayflower quickly was filling up with local spelling champions from all over the country. Each was accompanied by a reporter who, like myself, was supposed to keep the folks back home well informed on the week-long event. Considering that most contestants were about twelve years old, the stakes were high: $1,000 in cash and an appearance on the Ed Sullivan Show.

Unfortunately, Steve was knocked out in the second day of the bee. He was foiled by the word "amaryllis," a garden flower that obviously didn't grow in his backyard. But by that time, he, his mother, and I were having such a good time that we didn't much care.

"If I ever see an amaryllis, I think I'll stomp it out," Steve said philosophically.

Unlike many contestants and sponsors, the Markowskis and I hadn't spent all of our time studying difficult spelling words. We had become much more interested in calling room service, ordering elegant dinners, and jumping in and out of taxicabs. It was my first experience at staying at a truly fine hotel and I loved it. It's a feeling of excitement I never lost. Years later, when I was working at the *Inquirer*, I always volunteered for assignments in cities where no one else wanted to go. To me, a Holiday Inn in Dubuque, Iowa, is just as much fun as a Holiday Inn in New York City.

On the final night of the spelling bee, there was a huge

awards banquet. I dressed carefully for the ceremonies, slipping into the only dress in my suitcase that I hadn't worn yet. I looked in the mirror and congratulated myself on how chic and sleek I had become in five short days. I figured it was only a matter of time before the Washington *Post* scooped me up.

I took the elevator down to the grand ballroom, where I was supposed to meet the Markowskis. As I was waiting, a waiter came up and asked how I had ranked in the bee.

"Oh, you mean our champion," I said. "Well, he came out thirty-second."

"Your champion?" he replied. "I thought you were a contestant yourself—you look about twelve years old."

So much for chic and sleek.

By the time I had several years' experience behind me at the *Inquirer*, I was traveling quite a bit on national stories. I'm not sure the reason had anything to do with competence. I think the editors were simply overjoyed that they had found someone who showed boundless enthusiasm about trucking off to cities such as Cleveland, Ohio.

Now, before anyone thinks that I am being condescending, I want it fully understood that I love Cleveland. So what if most people don't? If the truth must be known, I enjoyed one of the most romantic weekends of my life there. Cleveland's main problem is that it can't seem to shake a long-standing reputation as a dull, drab, listless town. But then neither can Philadelphia. So who am I to criticize?

The first time I went to Cleveland was in November 1974, to cover a criminal suit brought against eight National Guardsmen who opened fire during the infamous student demonstrations at Kent State University in 1970. The four-year delay in getting the case into the courtroom had caused shock and disgust to fester into bitterness and despair. Four student protesters had been killed during the incident. But no one had ever been held responsible for their deaths.

Before I got involved in the story, I had few doubts that the guardsmen should be severely punished for killing the unarmed students. After all, hadn't the guardsmen's presence on the Kent campus during the protest of the United States invasion of Cambodia been a pure political scheme to enhance President Nixon's chances for reelection? And hadn't the guardsmen severely harassed the students during their peaceful demonstration? And hadn't the guardsmen opened fire and killed their young victims in cold blood? Well, hadn't they?

The answers to these questions were not quite so simple. When I began listening to testimony at the trial, I found that the circumstances were much less black and white than I had thought. The guardsmen, most of whom were the same age as the students, seemed to be victims too. The real guilty parties were nowhere in sight: the higher-up government officials who had ordered the inexperienced troops onto the Kent campus to teach a lesson to the young protesters. The men truly responsible successfully had passed the buck to their underlings.

The defendant who impressed me most was James Pierce, who was twenty-five years old when he was called onto the campus with his National Guard unit that fatal weekend. Pierce had been attending Kent part-time while fulfilling his military obligation. He never wanted to march onto the sprawling, green campus. He never wanted to be forced into a confrontation with his schoolmates. He never wanted to carry a gun. Yet, in some horrible twist of fate, Pierce ended up being accused of opening fire on the unarmed students.

After the bloody incident Pierce began getting obscene phone calls, which forced him to move from Ohio to New York. He later moved to Florida, where he was living when he was criminally indicted in the shooting. The firm he was working for promptly fired him.

"I have no idea where I'll find a job," Pierce told me during a recess of the trial. "I guess I'll just have to try to start over."

During the proceedings Pierce was not permitted by his attorney to discuss actual events: he could not say whether he did or did not recall firing his rifle. But in many respects that question seemed strangely irrelevant. Why should the young guardsmen have to take responsibility for an incident they had little control over? Shouldn't the men in authority—perhaps President Nixon himself—be the ones held accountable?

The judge apparently had his doubts about the case too. He ordered it dismissed because of lack of evidence against the defendants.

But the Kent State story—and my involvement—was not yet over. About six months later, in the spring of 1975, proceedings began on a civil suit brought by the parents of the four students who had been killed and the nine students who had been injured during the demonstration. The parents were asking $46 million in damages for the losses suffered by themselves and their families. This time, the defendants included the governor of Ohio, the former president of Kent State, and high-ranking National Guard officials.

Although the *Inquirer* did not cover the eight long weeks of testimony at the civil trial, they sent me to hear the final summations and await the verdict at the federal courthouse in Cleveland. The case was complicated and highly controversial, involving maps, photographs, ballistics test results, and conflicting testimony. The jury deliberated almost forty hours.

During those hours the scene at the courthouse was one of the most heart-wrenching I ever have experienced. In a room on one side of the courtroom sat the parents, whose emotional wounds had been ripped open once again during the upsetting testimony about their children's deaths and injuries. In a room across the hall sat the defendants, who scrupulously avoided meeting the eyes of their accusers.

On the first day of the jury deliberations, Mrs. Sarah Scheurer, whose daughter, Sandra, had been killed at Kent State, dabbed at her eyes with a lace handkerchief. She rarely stopped crying all week.

"I don't know what was worse—this waiting or actually seeing the guard who killed my daughter face to face in the courtroom," Mrs. Scheurer said. "I think only a mother who has lost a child can understand what you go through."

I didn't know what to say. To be sure, I knew well the pain and anguish of learning that a loved one suddenly had been killed. And that I never would see her again. And that I was totally defenseless in my grief. But I think the death of a parent cannot be compared with the death of a child. No mother ever expects her daughter to die first; it seems to defy all laws of nature.

"I just wonder if this ever is going to end," Mrs. Scheurer said.

As the days wore on and the jury still had not reached a verdict, I became more and more sympathetic to the plight of the parents. I tried hard to present the issues fairly in the daily stories I telephoned to the *Inquirer*, but I was deeply touched by numerous behind-the-scenes vignettes: Mrs. Florence Scroeder, whose son, William was killed, holding hands tightly with her husband; Mrs. Doris Krause, whose daughter, Alison, was dead, describing the night she identified the body at the morgue; Mrs. Elaine Holstein, who lost her son, Jeffrey, expressing her fears that the government apparently had the license "to shoot anybody."

Among the students who had been injured in the Kent incident was Dean Kahler, a pleasant, red-haired youth whose lifelong ambition had been to become a football coach. That ambition had been snuffed out when a guardsman's bullet struck him in the spine and paralyzed him from the waist down. Yet he worked hard at buoying up the spirits of everyone else.

"There is no way of ever assessing my own loss. Let's face it, I'll never walk again," Kahler said at the conclusion of the testimony. "I'm just glad that we finally got this case to the courtroom where we told the truth as well as we could. Now it's up to the jury to decide."

Unfortunately for Kahler and the other plaintiffs, the jury did not decide in their favor. None of the parents received a single cent to compensate them for their suffering. It almost was too much for some of them to bear.

"My God, I don't believe this," gasped Arthur Krause. Alison's father, when the verdict was announced after five days of deliberations.

"Murderers, murderers, you're all murderers," another spectator yelled at the jury.

Although I personally was shocked at the verdict, I

realized that my professional responsibility was to report the facts, not opinions. At any rate, I had no time to wallow in my own feelings. After sitting in the courthouse for almost a week with little to do but wait, I now was faced with the usual situation: only thirty minutes until deadline. I raced downstairs to the telephone.

Before placing my call, I scribbled down the lead, which is the first paragraph of a story. I followed the traditional news-writing formula: relating all the important facts first so readers would know the verdict right away.

I talked first to Jim Davis, the *Inquirer*'s assistant national editor, who transferred me to Murray Dubin, one of the *Inquirer*'s finest reporters. Murray's job was to type my dictation, a mundane task that most reporters, including myself, resent and complain bitterly about. But not Murray. He showed incredible patience as I dictated practically the whole story off the top of my head, frequently asking him to strike out one paragraph and insert another. He was a saint.

When it appeared in the paper, the story, as it should, gave no indication of my personal feelings, which I saved for a later analysis piece. The straight news story began:

CLEVELAND—National Guardsmen, Ohio Gov. James A. Rhodes, and other officials are not financially liable in the 1970 shooting at Kent State University, a federal jury ruled here yesterday.

After almost 40 hours of deliberations, a six-man, six-woman jury decided in favor of the defendants in a $46 million civil damages suit brought by the parents of the four students who were killed and the nine students who were wounded five years ago. The jury vote was 9 to 3. . . .

But to me, the Kent State decision seemed not a miscarriage of justice but an outright abortion; the only people who had paid a price for the shootings were the youngest and the most lowly: the guardsmen and the students. The officials responsible for calling the troops onto the troubled campus had paid nothing. I broke a long-standing practice of mine never to express an opinion to the principals in any lawsuit. I told Arthur Krause I thought the verdict smelled.

One of my longest-running out-of-town stories occurred strictly by accident. In October 1974 I went to Boston for the weekend to visit some friends. On Monday, shortly before I was planning to leave, the city erupted in widespread racial violence over the issue of court-ordered busing of schoolchildren.

I immediately called Steve Seplow, national editor at the *Inquirer*, to let him know I was right on the scene.

"Well, you may as well stay," Steve said. "Get a room and cover it for us."

Getting a room wasn't so easy. Because I already had said good-bye to my friends, I didn't want to impose anymore on their hospitality. But most of the city's hotels already were booked up with conventions and traveling businessmen. After making about a dozen calls, I finally got a room at the Parker House in downtown Boston. It was the last single available; a tiny cubicle that appeared crowded with only a small bed and a small bureau.

"Oh, well, I won't be here too long," I told the apologetic desk clerk.

That's what I thought.

On Tuesday Boston experienced its worst outbreak of violence since busing was ordered three weeks earlier to achieve racial integration in public schools. Thirty-three persons were injured, including one white taxicab driver who was beaten almost to death by some black youths. The attack apparently was made in retaliation for a similar assault the day before on a black motorist.

Although city officials kept schools open, only 69 percent of Boston's students showed up for classes that morning. The attendance figures at South Boston High School were even more dramatic: out of the 388 blacks scheduled to be bused to the formerly all-white school, only one braved the hostile crowds. Court order notwithstanding, black students clearly were not welcome in white schools.

The reverse situation also was true. About noon, the rumor control center at Boston City Hall reported that there had been a new outbreak of violence at English High, a formerly predominantly black school now being integrated by whites. I got in my rental car and drove over there. As I approached, I saw a group of parents, both black and white, tensely awaiting afternoon dismissal.

"How long can you expect kids to be patient with so much hatred going around?" one black social worker said. "They feel they have to retaliate against Whitey."

On Wednesday I ventured into South Boston, the all-white neighborhood most vigorously opposed to court-ordered busing. The residents, many of them natives of Ireland, welcomed me as one of their own. As a child of Irish-born parents, I could fully understand the white immigrants' fear and loathing that blacks soon would surpass them socially and economically. But while I understood the roots of the prejudice, I hated its flourishing growth.

"They [blacks] stay in their place down South," one South Boston wife told me. "There wouldn't be any trouble here if they would just stay where they belong."

Disturbed though I was by such sentiments expressed by adults, I even was more upset when I heard similar comments from children. Rather than stamping out the weeds of racial bigotry, many white parents seemed to be fertilizing their own fears through their children. One white boy named Chuckie told me his mother hadn't permitted him to go to school because she didn't want him sitting in the same classroom as black children. So, instead of attending classes, he was spending precious learning hours playing marbles.

"I wouldn't mind going to school myself, though," Chuckie said. "I like to beat up on the coloreds."

That afternoon I covered a special federal-court hearing to consider a request from black community leaders for increased police protection at newly integrated schools. As the judge was deliberating on the matter, the sound of police sirens and fire-engine whistles blared into the courtroom from the streets below. I wished desperately that I could be two places at once.

"I think I need help," I told Steve when I talked to him on the phone shortly after the judge had approved the blacks' request.

"Okay," Steve said. "Warren Brown is on his way."

Warren showed up later that evening. I don't think I was ever so happy to see reinforcements. Because Warren is black, we decided that he would have much greater access in the black community than I. Ordinarily, I question the wisdom of limiting black reporters to black stories as much as I oppose always assigning women reporters to women's stories. But in this particular situation, a division of labor along racial lines seemed sensible.

"I'm not about to go into South Boston anyway," Warren joked.

The following day, about three hundred state and federal troops were assigned to protect the forty-four black students who showed up for the first time at South Boston High. It seemed both grotesque and tragic that the heavily armed police outnumbered the pupils by more than six to one.

"South Boston used to be a nice place, but there are no Irish left," one eighty-year-old Irish man spluttered as the students were dismissed from school. "Everywhere the colored go, they wreck everything."

A few hours later, I telephoned the story into the *Inquirer*. During my conversation with Steve I mentioned that I had run into a serious problem.

Steve expressed concern. "Are you frightened? Were you threatened? Is there a lot of violence?"

"No, worse than that," I replied. "I don't have any clean clothes."

Because I had intended to visit Boston only for the weekend, I had been wearing the same two sets of clothing for four days. My one sweater was getting not only dirty but also downright offensive. Steve told me to go out and buy a change of clothing, courtesy of the *Inquirer*.

That evening Warren and I decided to go out together for dinner. I laughingly suggested that we go to a restaurant in South Boston, walking hand-in-hand.

"Are you crazy?" Warren said. "I don't want to be lynched."

On Friday the city's emotional heat finally began to cool. Boston officials reported one of the few positive stories that had developed all week: a group of black football players had rescued two white girls who were being beaten by a gang of thirty black thugs. Boston Mayor Kevin H. White personally visited the young athletes to extend his thanks.

In explosive situations such as Boston's busing controversy, the news media frequently is criticized for fanning the flames by reporting only negative stories. Not so with the *Inquirer*, at least in this case. The editors gave the football story one of the biggest page-one headlines all week.

On Saturday Steve told me to come back to Philadelphia. Much as I had enjoyed the challenge of covering the busing story, I was glad to leave. I was beginning to think that if I had to hear another white bigot vent his racial prejudices, I would punch him right in the mouth.

Although Kent State and Boston busing were among my most significant out-of-town assignments, my most memorable experience resulted from a short visit to a small upstate Pennsylvania town named Blanchard, population 500. In August 1975 I read a short item on the Associated Press wire noting that residents of the town had petitioned the state Department of Health to set up a massive extermination program to control a growing bat problem.

The situation seemed a natural for a light, entertaining story on "a town gone batty." It was. After driving one hundred miles to the tiny village, I quickly met a sixty-one-year-old gentleman who was so plagued by bats that he kept a badminton racquet in every room. He was more than happy to talk and demonstrate his technique for pulling the pesky rodents from the rafters of his home. At the end of a long day I felt that I had obtained a surefire "reader," which is what *Inquirer* editors call an interesting, if not significant, feature story.

Because I had wanted to see the bats myself, I had stayed in Blanchard far later than I normally would. So instead of driving to Philadelphia that night, I decided to stay in a motel in nearby State College. J checked in about 10 P.M.

After eating a quick dinner, I went back to my room, thoroughly exhausted. I undressed and climbed into bed after turning on *The Tonight Show*. I dropped off to sleep during the opening of Johnny Carson's monologue.

The next thing I knew I heard a loud bell. I awoke from my bed with a start. My God, I thought, the motel is on fire. Without even grabbing my clothes, I ran to the terrace outside my room. I realized that the bell was the telephone ringing just as the door locked behind me. I was stark naked.

To say the least, I was faced with an embarrassing dilemma. There were only two choices: I could cower in a corner until morning when the maid came, or I could walk up to the night clerk and ask for a key. Although the lobby was about three hundred yards from my room, I decided to make a run for it. I said a prayer of gratitude that no one was around.

To put it mildly, the night clerk was taken aback when I appeared in the buff at his counter. Here he was, suddenly faced with the classic comic question: what do you say to a naked lady? And what's more, where do you look?

As the clerk stood swallowing hard, another hotel employee appeared with a blanket and, mercifully, put it around my shoulders. Before I had a chance to speak, the telephone started ringing behind the desk.

"I think that might be for me," I said.

It was. Wiley, who had worked late that night in his job as an editor at the Philadelphia *Daily News*, was returning a call I had made earlier.

"What's going on?" he asked. "How come it took you so long to answer the phone?"

I burst out laughing. I barely could tell him what had happened. The more I tried to explain, the harder I laughed.

"Well, maybe you should go back to your room," Wiley suggested.

Later that night I thought with some amusement of my first out-of-town assignment in Washington, when I had dressed so carefully at the Mayflower Hotel. And here I was in upstate Pennsylvania standing totally nude in a motel lobby.

I had come a long way, baby.

5--Television

The television anchorman was talking to a reporter on the scene of a massive fire at an oil refinery in Philadelphia. The station had just purchased some expensive electronic equipment that permitted them to broadcast live and they obviously wanted to get their money's worth.

The problem was that the reporter had just gotten to the refinery moments before the 6 P.M. news and he really didn't have much information to relate. So, after a few minutes of stilted small talk, he signed off with a remark that more than ten men were believed to have been burned to death in the blaze.

"Well, hang in there," the anchorman told the reporter at the end of the discussion. "And keep cool."

A few days later, the reporters at the *Inquirer* still were snickering about the anchorman's sick attempt at humor. The joke, we all agreed, was a classic illustration of how television news is so dreadful and why newspapers are so much better. Most newspaper writers hold this conversation every chance they get.

Invariably, we all agreed on a number of basic points: television news is shallow, showy, and superficial; anchormen usually are chosen not for their news ability but for their good looks and sex appeal; television reporters, often lacking the time to check their facts, frequently give misleading and inaccurate information.

"Okay," I said as we lambasted broadcast journalism. "So why are we all so jealous?"

Everyone looked at me blankly.

At this point in history I don't think that there is much doubt that television news is far inferior to newspapers when it comes to reporting on an issue in depth. But there is a very reasonable explanation: time. With the limited amount of frequencies existing today, most networks and local stations simply do not have the space to provide detailed reports on routine happenings.

But, unlike most print reporters, I believe television news is fast improving and undoubtedly is going to become better and better. Right now, broadcasting is only thirty years old and still is experiencing growing pains suffered by newspapers hundreds of years ago. But as more channels open up in the future, television probably will devote increased amounts of time to producing quality news programming. The show *Sixty Minutes* may well become *Twenty-four Hours*.

"No, you're wrong," one newspaper friend often told me. "Television stations are just interested in selling dog food."

"Look, I'm not saying that newspapers are going to be obsolete," I would say. "But television news definitely is getting better."

During these arguments with my newspaper colleagues, I always felt a little foolish coming to the defense of the broadcasting industry. After all, I always was telling my non-newspaper friends how inadequate television news is. From my point of view, at least.

Because of my own particular reverence for the written word, I prefer to obtain my news from writers Carl Bernstein and Bob Woodward than from Walter Cronkite. I prefer to gather editorial opinion from columnist James Reston than from an anonymous station manager. I prefer to get my laughs from the comic section than from the so-called humorous "kickers" that usually end most local news broadcasts.

Yet I am the first to admit that one of my favorite fantasies is to be a television anchorwoman. Who can explain it? While I may object to watching television news, I wouldn't object at all to being watched. But much to my chagrin, I blew my one big chance.

During my brief sixteen months at the *Courier-Post* in 1970 and 1971 I wrote a weekly column that I envisioned as a cross between Art Buchwald, Erma Bombeck, and Dear Abby. But it was not my literary talents that attracted the attention of most of my readers.

Like most columns, mine appeared each week in the same section of the paper with the same heading. It was accompanied each time with a picture that made me look like a cross between Jackie Onassis and Natalie Wood. In other words, the photograph didn't look a thing like me; I loved it. And it almost made my television fantasy come true.

One Wednesday night after my column had appeared, the phone rang as I was preparing home-cooked spaghetti for dinner. I licked some tomato sauce off my fingers and ran to pick up the receiver. The voice on the other end of the line identified himself as the program director of a Philadelphia television station.

"We're changing our news format to include more

New Jersey news and we're looking for some bright, new faces," he said. "We'd like to talk to you."

"Sure, sure," I said, thinking with dismay that my voice sounded terribly high-pitched and squeaky. "How about this Friday?"

For the next two days I daydreamed constantly about becoming a big TV star. I practiced lowering my voice so that I would sound as authoritative as David Brinkley. I practiced making amusing jokes so that I would be as witty as Lucille Ball. I practiced interviewing friends so that I would seem as skillful as a White House correspondent.

What I didn't practice was looking pretty.

A few months earlier, I had noticed that my four front teeth were turning very gray. Brushing didn't help. When I went to the dentist, he found that the nerves in my teeth were dead, probably as a result of my car accident several years earlier. He had suggested that I have them capped and I had agreed. But as I usually do in any situation that involves a dental chair, I had been putting off the procedure for several weeks. So my teeth were still gray.

At the time of my television interview, women just were beginning to make inroads in the broadcast news business. Barbara Walters was not yet official cohostess of *The Today Show*. Female anchorwomen still were a rarity on local stations around the country. The few women reporters who worked on television inevitably seemed to be blonde and beautiful.

But, like a fool, I wasn't a bit worried. The television director, after all, had liked my writing. He would certainly realize that my darkened teeth were not going to affect my outstanding reporting abilities. He would have enough sense to base his hiring decision on brains, not beauty. He would notice that I had exactly the kind of wit and personality he was looking for.

Was I ever stupid!

On the day of my interview I dressed in the conservative fashion always recommended by employers for job interviews: herringbone suit, sensible shoes, hair sleeked back in a knot. I probably would have done better to dress like Chiquita Banana, complete with flying hair, low-cut dress, and satin skirts. Before leaving my apartment I gathered together some of my best news clippings and then headed for the station. I was a half-hour early. The secretary told me to have a seat and wait.

About fifteen minutes later the news director strode into the reception room and greeted me warmly. He shook my hand, then put his arm around me, then guided me into his office. So far, so good.

The interview started off like gangbusters: the television executive was so open and free that I hardly had a chance to fit a word in edgewise. Leaning back in his well-stuffed swivel chair, the news director briefed me on the Big Plans he was making to revamp the local news shows: more stories, more action, more colorful features. In other words, more pizzazz.

Then he told me that I might be exactly the kind of reporter he was looking for: bright, lively, young. I was extremely flattered. And happy. And excited. So I had a natural reaction.

I smiled. It was a fatal mistake.

As soon as the television news director saw my teeth, his entire manner changed. In the space of a minute his attitude toward me went from warm to cool. I tried to explain nonchalantly that I was going to have my teeth capped in the next few weeks. That I really wouldn't look this bad. That, no kidding, I looked quite pretty on camera.

But it was too late. Within the next five minutes, the TV executive suddenly remembered another appointment and dismissed me with the classic line: "If we need you, we'll call you," he said, smiling with his, oh, so perfect teeth.

I didn't smile back.

Needless to say, the station never called. And I ended up at the *Inquirer*, where the editors couldn't have cared less if I didn't have a single tooth in my head.

During the next few years I decided that I probably wouldn't have been happy in broadcasting anyway. As my career at the *Inquirer* progressed, I decided that there was nothing so exquisite as the pleasure-pain of sitting down at the typewriter. Nothing so satisfying as arguing over every word with an editor—and sometimes winning. Nothing so uplifting as seeing a thoroughly researched story appear on page one of the paper.

But I still was curious. How would I look and sound on television? I found out in a strange way.

When I resigned from the *Inquirer* in the spring of 1976 to attend law school at the University of San Francisco, Wiley and I packed all of our possessions into a U-Haul truck and began our journey across the country. After ten days we arrived in California, the land of sun, fun, and golden opportunity. Within forty-eight hours, a thief stole the truck, which contained everything we owned but a change of underwear.

To say the least, I was distraught. I didn't know what to feel worse about: losing all my material possessions or all my personal mementos and souvenirs. The thief had gotten not only my furniture and clothing but also my family photos, my yellowed letters from my mother, my sixth-grade diaries. And, to make matters worse, the police said that was little chance of getting anything back.

For the next month I felt like a lost woman. The thief had stripped me not only of my present but also of my past. I was utterly helpless. So, apparently, were the police. For six weeks they didn't have a clue.

Finally, Wiley and I were notified that we had been the latest victims of a quarter-million-dollar burglary ring stretching from San Francisco to Los Angeles. The thief, a twenty-one-year-old drug addict, had made the mistake of selling our moving van and some of our possessions to two undercover policemen.

Because the burglary ring had affected so many victims, the police announced the recovery of many of the goods and subsequent arrests at a large press conference attended by two dozen newspaper and television reporters. For the first time in my life I was the interviewee rather than the interviewer.

"Miss Begley, could you tell us exactly how you discovered that your truck had been stolen?" one television reporter asked, thrusting a microphone under my chin.

"Say, Kathy, could you come over here and pose by the truck?" a television camerman asked.

"Could you tell our viewers your feelings right now?" another television reporter prodded.

I felt like a star.

That night Wiley and I planned our entire evening around the local news broadcasts. We were most anxious to see the 10 P.M. news on station KTVU in Oakland because one of their reporters had interviewed us extensively.

At 9:55 P.M. I settled down on our recently recovered

sofa to watch the news on our recently recovered television. I was a nervous wreck. As the newscast began, I anxiously picked at my fingernails. I nervously bit my lip. I worriedly twirled a piece of my hair.

And then my image burst onto the screen in full living color. I leaned forward, hanging on my every word. I couldn't believe what I saw and heard. My voice sounded good. My eyes, ears, and nose photographed well. And my teeth, long since capped, looked terrific.

I was so thrilled with myself that I didn't notice that they had edited out most of Wiley's participation in the interview.

"Hey, what happened to me?" Wiley pouted jokingly.

"I don't know," I replied with a big grin. "I guess they recognize broadcasting talent when they see it."

And to think, Philadelphia television could have had me!

6--Censorship

Bob Mooney, one of the *Inquirer's* veteran photographers, nervously moped his brow as we approached the door of a theater in one of the raunchier sections of downtown Philadelphia. Overhead, a huge red marquee proclaimed CITY'S FIRST LIVE NUDE SHOW.

"Calm down," I joked as Bob put away his handkerchief.

"Yeah, yeah, let's go in," Bob said.

As we entered the theater, I was dismayed to find myself staring into the eyes of about twenty men in the audience. I was more dismayed to find that they were all staring back. I hadn't realized that the entrance of the theater opened onto a small hallway right beside the stage instead of a lobby.

Happily I soon learned that I was not the object of the audience's attention. Pornographic movies were. The manager cleverly had run the films to keep his customers entertained until showtime.

"No wonder everyone is staring up here." I laughed as I caught sight of the four naked actors on screen.

Normally the *Inquirer* was not in the habit of writing

about nude shows, live or otherwise. But because this bold 1974 presentation was the city's "first" and reportedly was drawing unusually large crowds, the editors thought it might be worth some sort of story. It was.

After about ten minutes of films, the live show began. Because I was the only woman in the audience, I sat in the back of the theater, trying hard not to look obvious. Bob moved up closer to the stage to get a better view.

"Strictly from a photographer's standpoint, of course," he said with a wink.

The star of the production was a woman named Miss Modesty, who was anything but. An accomplished acrobat, Miss Modesty used parts of her anatomy to perform bizarre tricks. I was flabbergasted.

So was Bob. Pulling out his camera, he began taking photographs from his front-seat vantage point. Although he was trying to act casual, it didn't work. Even from my seat twenty rows away, I could hear the film rolling after every shot. So could Miss Modesty.

"Hey, get that pervert out of here," Miss Modesty screamed, stopping her act literally in midair. "You're not allowed to take photographs."

Bob said okay and put away his camera. Then he walked to the back of the theater to sit next to me. I slinked down farther in my seat, pretending not to know him.

"Get away from me, you pervert," I joked.

But Bob, who had faced a lot of difficult assignments in his thirty-odd years as a photographer, was not about to give up so easily. He slowly eased his camera out from beneath his coat and began shooting again. This time the manager heard the film rolling.

"I'm afraid you both will have to leave," the manager

said after tapping us on the shoulder. "We have strict regulations about pictures."

We didn't bother to argue in the theater. But when we reached the manager's office, I quickly explained that we weren't normal, run-of-the-mill perverts; we were from the *Inquirer* and we wanted to do a story on Miss Modesty's unique act. The manager, realizing the value of free publicity, suddenly became very friendly.

"I like to think of these shows as art," he said as I tried to keep a straight face. "Philadelphia needs something artistic like this."

As the manager was discussing his belief in art for art's sake, Miss Modesty herself appeared in the office. She also had some interesting views on her profession.

"I think the human body is a beautiful instrument," said Miss Modesty, who declined to tell me her real name. "I don't want to be thought of as a sex object; I much prefer to be thought of as a racehorse with good control."

I wasn't about to argue with that statement. As Miss Modesty talked, Bob busied himself taking more photographs. This time he received full cooperation from the star, who even invited us into her dressing room. After about an hour, we decided that we had enough pictures and information and we started to leave.

"Well, that was an interesting assignment," Bob said as we approached the door.

"Yeah, interesting," I replied, happy to get out into the sunlight and fresh air.

Suddenly Bob stopped dead in his tracks. His face turned ashen. He pointed at a man hurrying by the City's First Live Nude Show sign.

"What's the matter?" I asked, expecting Bob to faint at any moment.

"I think that man is my minister," he replied. "And I think he saw me."

To be sure, stories about acts such as Miss Modesty's present many problems for journalists. Running into the local minister isn't a frequent difficulty. But writing the story without getting obscene is.

When I got back to the city room, I was at a complete loss on how to describe Miss Modesty's act in a manner acceptable to the *Inquirer*'s standards as a "family" newspaper. According to these standards, followed by most of America's daily papers, stories should be suitable reading for even the youngest children in a subscriber's home.

Because I like to use description in my writing, I found it extremely hard to describe Miss Modesty's act in anything but terms more suitable for *Playboy* magazine than for the *Inquirer*. The editors agreed. Whatever I wrote, which is not fit for reprinting here either, was changed to the following:

In a series of sinewy choreographed routines, star Miss Modesty, who obviously devised her stage name with tongue in cheek, gave an acrobatic performance that stopped short only of swinging from the chandelier.

Much as I hated to admit it, I thought the rewritten version was pretty good.

Bob's photographs had an entirely different fate. In the first edition of the following day's paper, my story was accompanied by a full-length picture of Luscious Lisa, a bikini-clad dancer who followed Miss Modesty's act. The photograph, which showed Luscious in a slightly lascivious standing pose, apparently was too much for some of the editors. They cut Luscious Lisa off at the waist so that readers of later editions never had a chance to see her torso or legs.

"I think that's what you call hitting below the belt," I joked to a friend.

Whatever our editorial problems with Miss Modesty's story, the manager of the theater loved it. He didn't even get angry when the police closed down the show a few days after the piece appeared. The manager correctly figured that the publicity would double the audience when he eventually reopened.

A few days after the interview I was surprised to find a large bouquet of flowers on my desk, sent by Miss Modesty and her manager. Ordinarily reporters don't accept gifts from sources, but I felt that flowers would be a little difficult to send back. I put them in a vase and placed them in the center of the city room.

Considering that Miss Modesty and the manager initially had not wanted to cooperate with photographs and interviews, I found it rather amusing that they had later sent the flowers. Then I thought about Miss Modesty's comment about wanting to be thought of as a racehorse.

So who's going to look a racehorse in the mouth?

Coincidentally, that same year I also became involved in another assignment of questionable good taste. This time I was sent to interview a stripper who called herself Zsa Zsa Gaborr, much to the consternation of the Hungarian actress, who spells her last name with one *r*. Zsa Zsa was appearing at the Troc, an oldtime burlesque house in Philadelphia.

Unlike Miss Modesty, Zsa Zsa had little or no acrobatic ability. On the contrary, her act consisted mostly of disrobing slowly while executing a few rather stiff boxsteps. But the crowd at the Troc was not interested in watching Zsa Zsa dance. They were interested in watching her reveal her heavily advertised seventy-three-inch breasts.

To put it mildly, I had mixed feelings about the assignment. On the one hand, I didn't want to promote an act that I considered terribly demeaning to women. On the other hand, I didn't want to rule out the possibility that I could obtain an interview that would provide insight into why a woman would take such a humiliating job.

When I arrived at the theater, Zsa Zsa was just winding up her act. It was some act. Because of her truly mammoth mammaries, she seemed to have great difficulty just moving, much less dancing around the stage.

"It's harder for her to move than for normal girls," the manager snickered. "She gets a lot of backaches and all."

After the show Zsa Zsa bounced offstage and headed for her dressing room, which was distinguished by a big red star marked in crayon on the door. She stopped for a moment to check her hairdo in a mirror plopped atop a bunch of overflowing trash bags.

"I have to go shopping this afternoon," she told the manager when he told her I was there to conduct an interview. "I don't have time to talk to a reporter."

That was just fine with me. I didn't want to sit around backstage in an artificial interview situation either. As a reporter I long since had learned that subjects are much more natural and open when they're doing something ordinary or routine. Shopping was a natural.

"I'd love to go along," I said, breathing a sigh of relief when Zsa Zsa didn't object.

As Zsa Zsa changed into her street clothes, I talked

with her inside her dressing room, which was illuminated by a single lightbulb dangling from the ceiling, Politely looking away, I wondered if she had problems buying clothes to fit her full figure. When I saw her outfit, I didn't bother to ask. Her everyday clothes consisted of a pair of slacks, a loose-fitting man's sweater, and a large pea coat, with the buttons popped off.

"Zsa Zsa almost looks normal with her clothes on," the manager said.

Which is more than could be said about her friend Bubbles, who accompanied us on the shopping spree. Bubbles, also a professional stripper, was about six feet tall and wore a skirt that ended not more than six inches below her hips. Her hair, teased into a flaming red mass atop her head, looked as if it had been coiffed by a construction crew.

As the three of us headed outside, I was tempted to call my editor to see if there was a photographer available to capture the shopping spree on film. But I had been told earlier that the picture department already was over-scheduled that day. So I didn't bother. But to this day, I would give anything to have a photograph of me with Zsa Zsa and Bubbles posing in front of Independence Hall. We were truly a sight for sore eyes.

At first my two stripper friends and I browsed through a few novelty stores, where Zsa Zsa bought several trinkets for her two children. After about an hour, Bubbles said she was going to go off on her own to buy some back-to-school outfits for her kids. Zsa Zsa invited me to accompany her to the African Feather Shop.

"The African Feather Shop?" I said in surprise. "I've lived in Philadelphia most of my life and I've never heard of it."

Little wonder. As it turned out, the store was located

atop an old warehouse and could be reached only on a rickety, old caged elevator. The outside of the shop, marked by a small, faded, almost unreadable sign, looked totally drab and lifeless. But the inside was something else altogether; an entire factory floor was filled with feathers of every conceivable size and description. Zsa Zsa acted like a child in a Christmas shop.

"Do you like this one?" Zsa Zsa said, wrapping herself in a black feather boa. "Or do you think it's too dark for my skin?"

As she pranced around in an assortment of feathered costumes, Zsa Zsa began to tell me about her life. In brief, it consisted of a Jewish childhood in Germany, extermination of her family by Nazis, flight to Israel, marriage to a Brooklyn meatcutter, birth of two daughters, murder of her husband during an armed holdup in a butcher shop.

I didn't believe a word of it. But I don't think Zsa Zsa expected me too. It was a well-rehearsed tale.

When I asked Zsa Zsa if she felt that she was being exploited as a stripper, she said definitely not.

"I've supported this body of mine for years," she said, laughing at her own joke. "It's about time it supported me for a change."

As we walked back to the theater, however, Zsa Zsa made it quite clear that she was willing to accept money for stripping but "not for anything else." Then she pointed to her left ring finger. She was wearing a thin gold wedding band. It was, she said, strictly for protection.

"Men are all the same," she said.

When I got back to the city room, I wrote what I

thought was one of my more sensitive articles, depicting Zsa Zsa as a woman trapped in a world of heavy breathing, snide remarks, and cheap theaters. It never ran. What ran instead was a rewritten version describing Zsa Zsa's breasts as "an awesome statement on mother love and woman lust." I hated it. The editors wanted to put my byline on it with that of another reporter. I said no.

About a year later, God knows why, the editors decided to send me on yet another strip story. This one involved a club that featured go-go boys just outside Washington, D.C. Once again the idea of the piece was to provide insight into why such clubs were becoming so popular. Once again my article didn't exactly fit the standards of a family newspaper.

In writing the story I made the same unforgivable mistake that I had made in writing the story about Miss Modesty. I described the act, which included a lot of prancing and seminudity by some well-endowed male dancers. The story was killed, which means exactly what it sounds like. It never appeared in the paper at all.

"I wish they'd stop sending me to these places," I told my editor, Max King. "I bet some of the editors must think I have a sick mind."

"Well," Max said with a wry smile, "next to them, you probably do."

At the *Inquirer*, when any story was killed before publication, word spread like fire around the newsroom. This case was no different. One by one, my fellow reporters came by my desk to offer their sympathy and condolence. Ellen Karasik, who was one of the first respected woman news reporters at the paper, had her own theory on the subject.

"I think it's significant that they killed a story about male go-go-dancers," she said. "I mean, we've run hundreds of articles about female dancers."

Much as I would have loved to believe there was some sexist implication in the rejection of my story, I had to admit in truth that I didn't think so. Ellen, of course, had no way of knowing my past history on stories involving nudity and strippers.

The truth of the matter was that I like to write it how I see it. And what I saw on these kinds of stories was not exactly a Walt Disney movie.

Having struck out three times, I vowed to myself that I would never again write a story about any kind of semipornographic act. And, if asked, I would pull out a sign saying, "I Do Not Cover Dirty Stories."

My rationale would be the same as maids and butlers who refuse to do dirty floors and windows. They are too hard to make clean.

7--Miss America

Bob Greenberg, then city editor of the *Inquirer,* said he had a good story for me. Although Bob always hyped up stories to arouse enthusiasm in his reporters, I fell for the bait every time. I got excited.

"How would you like to cover the Miss America Pageant this year?" Bob asked.

I gulped hard. I honestly didn't know how to answer.

Like most little girls who grew up in the 1950s and 1960s, I spent a lot of my adolescence dreaming about one day becoming Miss America. Every year at pageant time, I would scrutinize the contestants' faces on television, looking for someone who had full cheeks or freckles or brown hair that even faintly resembled mine. I never found anyone. But this did not prevent me from crying tears of joy every time Bert Parks announced a new winner.

By the time I was twelve years old, I realized that my dream was hopeless; that I never was going to be pretty enough to win the Miss America title. But I still watched the show faithfully every fall on television, and I still cried my eyes out each time a new queen was crowned. Only I no longer was shedding tears of joy for the winner but tears of self-pity for myself. I knew I never was going to make it to the Miss America Pageant.

Little did I know.

By the time I was old enough to enter the contest, my face had thinned out, my freckles had disappeared, and my hair had grown long and lustrous. But by this time I had absolutely no desire to enter any sort of beauty contest. It was then the late 1960s and no self-respecting feminist would be caught dead parading around in a bathing suit before a panel of almighty judges.

Like most newspapers, however, the *Inquirer* continued to cover the pageant year after year with the solemnity usually afforded only to presidential elections. But why not? Everyone in television knows that the Miss America always gets one of the largest annual viewing audiences. So newspaper executives undoubtedly felt that seriously covering the Big Event also would sell a few extra papers. And it probably did.

The economics of it all, of course, was of little concern to me. By 1971, the year the *Inquirer* asked me to cover it, I believed that the Miss America Pageant was exploitative, insulting, and degrading to women. And I couldn't imagine why the paper wanted me to get involved with it.

"I think the whole pageant is a bunch of garbage," I told a friend when I was muddling over my decision of whether to go to the competition.

"Exactly why you should cover it," my friend said. "You could put a new slant on things."

Ordinarily I would have recoiled at the mere idea of "slanting" a story. A reporter's duty is to report both sides of any issue, no matter what his or her opinion. But in this case I thought that the Miss America Pageant had been promoted for years from only one side: one brimming with virtue, beauty, and mushy apple pie. Few reporters ever had written about the other side: one brimming with commercialism, ugliness, and spiked apple cider. I decided to give it a try.

Like most television viewers, I always had thought of the pageant as a one-night affair. Nothing could be further from the truth. Although the only televised portion of the pageant occurs Saturday night, the competition actually begins the Sunday before with a reception during which contestants get their first chance to size up the opposition, to count how many girls are prettier than they, and to plan their battle strategy. It is a strange welcome.

After I had checked into my hotel, I went over to the Atlantic City Convention Bureau to pick up my official press packet. Inside was a staggering amount of information on each girl in the pageant. With a single glance a reader could find out which contestant was the shortest, which contestant was the oldest, and which contestant had the biggest breasts.

And that was not all. The packet also contained a thirty-six-page booklet outlining the official "precepts of conduct" for both contestants and the press. In no uncertain terms, the beauty queens were cautioned not to drink, not to smoke, not to appear at any parties in public. The reporters were warned not to speak to any of the girls without their official chaperone, not to ask controversial questions, not to approach contestants except at especially designated times. I could not believe my eyes.

In any normal situation the press always vigorously opposes any coverage "rules" as an infringement of the

First Amendment. But the Miss America Pageant clearly was not a normal situation. Most of the newspaper people covering the event not only obeyed the rules but also agreed with them. I soon discovered why.

Unlike most national stories the Miss America Pageant does not attract reporters from news giants such as the Los Angeles *Times* or the Chicago *Tribune*. Most of the people on the beauty contest beat come from small towns in Indiana or Iowa or Kansas where the entire community feels a personal interest in the outcome. Not coincidentally, many of the newspapers in these areas actually sponsor the local competitions and so have quite an investment in the final event. So what reporter is going to complain, especially when he or she is getting an expense-paid visit to the East Coast as part of the assignment?

On Monday the contestants began rehearsals for the musical production numbers that open every pageant. As Indian-summer temperatures soared into the nineties, the young beauty queens sang and danced and mimicked their way through endless practice sessions in the stifling performance hall. And, contrary to their images, most of the girls wound up the day with soggy underarms, wilted hairdos, and very sore feet.

On Tuesday it was more of the same. Except that after a grueling day of rehearsals, the contestants were required to dress in their high-school-prom best and to ride on floats in the annual boardwalk parade. As always, most of the girls put petroleum jelly between their gums and their lips so their mouths wouldn't get chafed from smiling so much.

The preliminary competitions opened on Wednesday and continued through Friday. During this time the group was divided into three sections; each third competed every day in one of three categories: swimsuit, evening gown, and talent. The swimsuit event, during which the girls presented several full-body profiles for scoring by the judges, always received the loudest applause from the audience.

All of which drove a lot of feminists nuts.

On Friday a group called Radical Women began picketing outside Convention Hall with signs saying, "Atlantic City is the seat of oppression with a pair of panties" and "Miss America is a bust with a brassiere on." As I was interviewing one of the demonstrators, another walked up and asked me why I was covering the pageant.

"Are you crazy or something?" she asked in a thick Brooklyn accent.

I was beginning to wonder.

All through the week I had been trying to write perceptive articles that would depict the Miss America Pageant not as a serious news event but as one of the most successful promotional stunts in world history. Instead of emphasizing the figures of the contestants, I tried to emphasize the figures in the account books of Atlantic City's hotels and restaurants; the pageant originally was devised, after all, to give local innkeepers one more week of business after Labor Day.

But try as I might to downplay the competitive, sexist aspects of the contest, I was not entirely successful. *Inquirer* readers began to call in and complain that they couldn't adequately measure up the young beauty queens without their vital measurements.

"If they want their measurements so bad, let them come down here with a tape measure," I told an editor when he mentioned the complaint to me over the phone.

By Saturday night almost everyone in Atlantic City

had a bet riding on the winner. Most of the girls had been assigned specific handicaps, depending on breast size, leg shape, and fanny overhang. The atmosphere was exactly like a racetrack.

"I'll give two-to-one odds on Miss Idaho," one reporter said to another.

"Nah, her body's awful," said the second guy, balancing his notebook on his beer belly.

By the time the winner was announced, I had practically given up all hope of writing a really top-notch story. But I thought I'd put in one last try. When the winner, an Ohio girl named Laurie Lea Schaefer, was crowned Miss America, I approached her for an interview. The most significant thing she said was that she was "thrilled and happy" and that she liked to make fondues. I wrote a feature story attempting to highlight the absurdity of it all. But the *Inquirer*, reverting to its old ultra-serious coverage, ran a front-page story similar to the kind written to announce the end of a world war. It said:

> Laurie Lea Schaefer, 22, of Bexley, Ohio, was crowned Miss America today in Atlantic City, N.J.
>
> The 22-year-old auburn-haired graduate of the University of Ohio won the competition over four other finalists including Miss Pennsylvania, who finished fourth.
>
> "I'm so thrilled and happy," the new Miss America said backstage immediately after the crowning. "I just can't believe it."
>
> The new Miss America won the swimsuit competition Friday night. She is 5 foot 7 and measures 36-24-36. Her talent was classical singing.

The story went on and on, each paragraph worse than

the one before. It was exactly the kind of article I had avoided writing all week. And, worst of all, it had my name on top of it. I vowed that I never would go to the Miss America Pageant again.

But I did, the very next year. I still don't know why. The contest almost was an exact repeat of the year before; and what was worse, so was the *Inquirer*'s coverage. Once again the editors managed to insert the contestants' measurements into most of my stories.

I was furious.

"Look, it's basically a question of good journalism," I argued. "You guys never would give this kind of coverage to an ordinary publicity event, if it didn't involve beautiful girls."

By 1973 the editors at the *Inquirer* had begun to see my point of view. But it had nothing to do with me. Earlier that year Gene Roberts, the former national editor of the New York *Times*, took over the reins of the *Inquirer* and decided to make it one of the finest papers in the country. And the finest papers in the country had long since abandoned serious coverage of the Miss America Pageant.

A full month before the competition in Atlantic City, one of the editors suggested that I do an in-depth article on preparations being made by the directors of the Miss Pennsylvania Pageant. I regarded the story as one of my finer hours. It appeared the day the finals began.

Ben Bronstein smacked his lips, wiped the perspiration from a few strands of hair painstakingly combed over his bald spot and said he thought 18-year-old Tina Louise Thomas was "a magnificent thing."

"What a great body," Bronstein said, rolling his

eyeballs appreciatively at Tina Louise Thomas. "I'll tell you, if she doesn't win the swimsuit division, I'd like to see the body that does."

Tina Louise Thomas is representing Pennsylvania in this year's Miss America Pageant, which begins today in Atlantic City.

Last week, about 75 state contest officials showed up at the Hershey Community Theater for final inspection of "our girl" and her new $5,000 wardrobe, and most seemed as delighted as Bronstein.

"I think we've got a winner this time," one pageant official said after Miss Thomas modeled a series of form-fitting gowns. "She looks a lot better than she did in the state pageant. They really worked on her."

Although pageant officials had been discussing methods of selling their contestants for years, the Miss Pennsylvania group was not too happy to see their behind-the-scenes statements appear in the newspaper. They quickly forgot about all the favorable free publicity they had received from the *Inquirer* for more than fifty years; they decided I was out to get them. Ben Bronstein never spoke to me again.

Before I left for my third annual trip to Atlantic City, the editors and I decided that I at long last could skip the routine preliminary competitions and interviews. My mission was to write about the little-known peculiarities of the Miss America Pageant. And there were plenty to write about.

My most successful story was coverage of one of the nightly parties that occur throughout the week. To my knowledge, unbelievable though it seems, it was the first time a reporter had covered any of the social events that abound at the pageant. It began:

ATLANTIC CITY—Dick London sat slumped at a table, a cigarette dangling from his left hand, and said he was getting tired of all the hoopla at the Miss America Pageant.

"All this drinking and partying is getting a little old," said London, a college student who acts as technical director for the Miss New Mexico Pageant. "Party, party, party, that's all anyone does."

Partying? And drinking? At the beauty pageant long known for its wholesome, goody-goody, girl-next-door image? London has got to be kidding.

Hardly. Although pageant officials never advertise the fact, the annual Miss America competition operates on an incredible double standard: all work for the contestants, all play for the adult sponsors.

In the official "Precepts of Conduct for Contestants," for example, the beauty queens are strictly forbidden to attend parties, smoke in public or imbibe alcoholic beverages.

No such precepts exist for the 20 to 30 state pageant officials who come here, often with bottle and glass in hand, to cheer on each girl through three long nights of preliminary competition, plus the final, which will be televised at 8:30 tonight.

"I haven't been sober since I got here," one bleary-eyed Connecticut official said.

Once again, the pageant officials were not exactly overjoyed at my reporting abilities. Neither were many of the reporters. I apparently was threatening everyone's good time.

The night the party story appeared, one of the dancers in the show cornered me in a hallway in one of Atlantic City's finest hotels. Without beating around the bush, he told me that I obviously was out to ruin American womanhood, that I had no respect for feminine beauty, and that, if I knew what was good for me, I had better get out of town—quickly.

The dancer's threats sounded so much like he had memorized them from an old *Gunsmoke* TV script that I almost burst out laughing. But I could easily see that he was in no laughing mood.

I simply walked away, saying nothing.

On Saturday night a pleasant-looking woman named Rebecca Ann King won the Miss America title. She was not, to put it mildly, the crowd's favorite.

"She's not even pretty," one reporter groaned when Bert Parks announced her selection.

Backstage, the new Miss America's father told me that he used to encourage his daughter to watch the pageant each year on television to "show her what other girls could do." He obviously was proud that his prodding had worked. The *Inquirer* ran the story of her victory, with her father's comments and without her vital statistics, exactly as I wrote it. Hooray!

The following morning I attended the traditional Sunday-morning brunch interview with the newly crowned Miss America. During the session Miss King, who had entered the contest as Miss Colorado, gave her opinions on various issues of importance in 1973. Yes, she said, she still supported Richard Nixon despite the Watergate scandal. No, she said, she didn't know how she would spend the $125,000 she was expected to earn from personal appearances. Yes, she said, she had once worked for Barry Goldwater.

In one corner of the room Miss America's father held his nineteen-month-old granddaughter, the child of Miss King's older sister. He said that he had dreams for her also.

"Isn't she beautiful, with her blue eyes and blond

hair?" he asked. "I'm sure she'll follow in the footsteps of her aunt Rebecca."

Considering the Miss America Pageant's past track record overcoming feminist criticism, it's likely that the contest will endure long enough for Miss America's niece to reach the eligible age, which should be in the 1990s. And I hope that, if that's what she really wants, she wins.

But at the same time I fervently hope also that no newspapers will cover her victory.

8--Watergate

It was spring of 1974 and the Watergate scandal was splashed across every newspaper in the country. It had been almost two years since the break-in at the Democratic National Headquarters in Washington, D.C., but hints of White House involvement were just beginning to leak out to the general public.

One of the earliest casualties of the Watergate affair was L. Patrick Gray, who had been nominated to succeed J. Edgar Hoover as the director of the FBI. Gray had been ruined during Senate confirmation hearings when he disclosed that he had delivered voluminous reports on the break-in to White House counsel John Dean.

When Congress made it quite clear that it had no intentions of confirming his appointment, Gray returned to practice law in his hometown of New London, Connecticut. He had been there for about a year when Steve Seplow, the editor who later directed my efforts during the Boston busing controversy, decided that Gray might be able to provide some background on what on earth was going on in Washington.

102

To Steve, one of the most dedicated newsmen at the *Inquirer*, it was entirely irrelevant that Gray had not given a single interview, had not made a single public appearance, had not attended a single community event since his return to private life.

My assignment, should I choose to accept, was to get an exclusive, firsthand account of what went on behind the Gray door. I chose to accept.

"Well, I'll try," I told Steve.

"Great," he said. "Now get out of here."

At that time in my career I had developed a reputation for my ability to obtain interviews when others had failed. It had nothing to do with questioning technique, writing skill, or reporting ability. I used a very direct approach: I simply showed up in a subject's home or office and caught them offguard. I did not believe in calling ahead.

In this particular case, of course, I realized that not setting up an appointment beforehand was risky. What if I traipsed all the way to Connecticut and discovered that Gray was vacationing in Florida? Or that he was quarantined with the measles? Or that he had moved to Alaska?

Despite my fears, however, I felt that showing up unannounced was a chance I had to take. Gray successfully had been avoiding interviews for more than a year. I believed that the only way I would be able to convince him to talk to me would be in person. It was too easy to hang up over the phone.

Before leaving, I photocopied the *Inquirer*'s clippings on Gray so that I could read them on the plane. I was glad Steve had decided not to send a photographer; the clips were so thick that I would have had no time for conversation. When I checked into my hotel that night in

New London, I jotted down a few key questions that I wanted to be sure and ask Gray. I felt totally confident.

The next morning I drove directly to the offices of Suisman, Shapiro, Wool and Brennan, where L. Patrick Gray worked. I noted with amusement that the former Nixon appointee no longer referred to himself by the same name. The sign on the law office now listed him as Gray, Louis P.

I walked into the firm's brightly decorated office and announced that I would like to see Mr. Gray as soon as possible. The secretary excused herself but returned a few minutes later.

"Sorry, Mr. Gray's appointments are completely full today," she said. "Why don't you call tomorrow?"

I was disappointed and relieved at the same time. On the one hand, I was sorry I couldn't get an appointment that afternoon. But, on the other, I was ebullient that Gray wasn't out of town.

Because I obviously wasn't going to get to first base that day, I decided to stroll around the rest of the playing field—the streets of New London. I often had found that I could pick up a lot of useful information by talking to the neighbors and friends of an interviewee.

In a hotel up the street a talkative waitress mentioned that Gray usually had the same thing every day for lunch, roast beef on white. In City Hall the tax collector said the entire town felt very sympathetic toward Gray's plight. In a local store the saleswoman said that Gray seemed to keep to himself ever since his fall from power. The tidbits of information were a start.

Next I decided to head for the local newspaper, the New London *Day*. The library had an entire drawer full of clippings on people named Gray. L. Patrick's were sandwiched between envelopes marked "Gray, Jessie, retires from phone company," and "Gray, William, breaks arm."

For the next four hours I read every story that the *Day* ever had printed about the onetime acting FBI director. I quickly learned that Gray, like most so-called overnight political successes, had been laying groundwork for years for his rise on the national scene. As early as 1960 he had campaigned actively for Richard Nixon.

"Gray used to be fairly accessible but no one has seen him in public since he came home from Washington," said Art Weber, city editor of the *Day*. "He's just not talking about Watergate, and that's it."

I winced. Hopefully I could change his mind.

After taking numerous pages of notes, I headed back to my hotel. Having eaten a marvelous stuffed-trout dinner in a local seafront restaurant, I decided to make the most of the remainder of the evening. I drove out to Gray's suburban home and knocked on the door.

No answer.

Darn, I thought to myself.

On my way back to the hotel I passed a brightly lit church with a sign advertising a community play. I got a sudden hunch that Gray might be in the audience. I parked in the lot nearby and strode toward the vestibule. My blind hunches on stories frequently turned out to be right.

This time they were dead wrong.

"We haven't seen Mr. Gray in months," a clergyman told me. "I'm sure I would have noticed if he had come here tonight."

Before going to bed, I called Steve at home. I tried to sound more optimistic than I felt.

"Just hang in there," Steve said.

The following morning I telephoned Gray's office as his

secretary had advised. She told me that she had given him my message about the interview.

"Well, may I set up an appointment?" I asked.

"Call back this afternoon," she said.

I was beginning to suspect I was getting the royal runaround. I decided the best course of action would be to go to Gray's office, plop myself in a chair, and wait. He had to come out sooner or later.

On my way up the two flights of stairs leading to the law firm's suite, I noticed a small room with a barber's sign outside. As I passed by, the proprietor waved at me with his hair clippers.

"Hi, there," I said, thinking the barber might tell me some anecdotes about Gray. "My name is Kathy Begley and I'm from the *Inquirer*."

As it happened, the barber was one of the best gossips in town. Although he didn't know anything about Gray's political background, he knew plenty about his personal life: what make of car he drove, what brand of clothes he wore, what kind of hours he worked. The only question he couldn't answer was whether Gray had been involved in the planning of the Watergate break-in.

"Well, I guess even the barber can't always know for sure," I joked.

When I finally walked into Gray's outer offices, it was close to 1 P.M. I told the secretary that I still wanted to make an appointment.

"Look, I think that if Mr. Gray wanted to see you, he would have called you back," she said, no longer beating around the bush.

"Well, maybe not," I said cheerfully. "I need only a few minutes of his time. I can wait."

As I settled myself into a chair, the secretary hurried

into a side hallway, presumably leading to Gray's office. She returned about ten minutes later.

"I'm afraid Mr. Gray has appointments all afternoon," she said. "I'm certain that he won't be available for hours."

"That's no problem," I said. "I'm in no hurry."

For the next two hours I remained in the same chair, reading and rereading the same magazines. Occasionally the secretary would tell me again that Mr. Gray was very busy. And I would tell her again that I was in no hurry.

By 4 P.M. I decided that it was time to use my only trump card. Steve had told me that one of the *Inquirer's* senior editors was an old friend of Gray's. Earlier, I had been reluctant to name-drop because I didn't really have permission. But now I was getting desperate.

"Look, I work with an old friend of Mr. Gray's," I told the secretary. "I'd at least like to give him his regards."

After the secretary rushed back to the rear offices again, I rationalized my little white lie. I mean, who would resent my conveying some innocent regards? I just hoped Gray wouldn't phone the senior editor, who didn't even know I was in Connecticut.

A few minutes later, Gray himself finally emerged from his office. Dressed in a well-tailored pin-stripe suit, he looked much more dapper than his photographs. Hoping that flattery would get me anywhere, I quickly told him so.

He was not impressed.

As I babbled on about my desire to write about his side of the Watergate story, Gray grabbed me firmly by the elbow. It quickly became apparent that he was planning to steer me right out the front door. I had to talk fast.

In rapid-fire succession I told Gray that the whole country was anxious to learn his opinion of the Nixon administration, that the *Inquirer* would present the issues fairly, and that I probably would kill myself if I had to go back to Philadelphia without a story. Nothing worked.

Gray was polite, but firm.

"It has been my policy all along not to give interviews," he said. "And I see no reason to change that policy now."

Although I was deeply disappointed that I didn't obtain the exclusive interview, I figured that I had enough background information to write an article about the town's reaction to the return of their onetime political hero. On the plane, I scribbled out the lead:

NEW LONDON, Conn.—Every 10 days, Louis P. Gray shows up in Garde's Barbershop here precisely at 8 a.m. and gets his hair trimmed exactly the same way he did during his 20 years in the Navy, one-quarter inch from the head.

Then Gray climbs two flights of stairs to the law offices of Suisman, Shapiro, Wool and Brennan and begins a day of work usually interrupted only by a brief lunch at the Mohican Hotel, a half block down the main street of this seaside town of 30,000 residents.

Precisely at 5 P.M., the 58-year-old lawyer walks three blocks to the $1-per-day municipal parking garage and gets into the compact car he bought recently to save gasoline on the 10-mile trip from town to his home in suburban Stonington. He and his wife, Beatrice, rarely go out in the evenings.

There is little about Louis P. Gray's mundane lifestyle as a small-town lawyer in southeastern Connecticut to suggest that he and L. Patrick Gray,

onetime Nixon aide and powerful acting director of
the FBI, are one and the same man.

Which is exactly the way Gray wants it.

Don't ask how, but I somehow stretched my material
into a 1,500-word article. It wasn't exactly a hard-hitting
story, but I was reasonably pleased. At least I had gotten
to see Gray face to face. I hadn't even managed that on
my first Watergate assignment.

In the summer of 1973 the Senate Watergate hearings
created an entire bevy of new television stars: Sam
Ervin, the bushy-browed senator from North Carolina;
Bob Haldeman, powerful aide to President Nixon;
Howard Baker, senator from Tennessee. But the greatest
celebrity of all was Maureen Dean, who appeared on TV
day after day, although she was not a principal in the
legal proceedings. Mrs. Dean's main claims to fame were
that she was married to John Dean, special counsel to the
President—and that she was beautiful.

During Dean's initial days of testimony during the
televised Ervin hearings, the cameras often focused on
Mrs. Dean. At the beginning of the week most journalists
were wondering who she was. By the end they were
wondering when they could interview her. She seemed to
be an obvious source for a story on the home lives of the
politically embattled President's men.

Despite the media interest, however, Mrs. Dean did not
begin scheduling interviews. On the contrary, she managed to avoid reporters as adeptly as Richard Nixon
himself. No wonder. Newspaper and television reporters
wanted her story for free. A book publisher later paid
her thousands of dollars for it.

Although I can sympathize with Mrs. Dean's right to

write about her own story, I wasn't too happy about it when Steve sent me to Washington to try and interview her. It was not exactly a novel idea; about two dozen other reporters were trying to do the same thing. It was hopeless; she did not answer the telephone or the doorbell at her home for weeks. There was no office to park myself in.

But I found some consolation about a year later when the *Inquirer* sent me to Washington again, this time to interview Rep. Charles Sandman of New Jersey. Although Sandman probably will end up at best as a small footnote in history, he was, for one shining moment, a celebrity worthy of having his craggy face emblazoned on T-shirts and his "des, dem, dose" manner of speaking imitated on *The Mike Douglas Show*. He was, in other words, a political Tiny Tim: here today, gone tomorrow.

At the time I met him in his Capitol Hill office, however, Sandman had attracted nationwide attention for his vigorous defenses of Nixon during the Watergate hearings. A relatively obscure congressman, the Jerseyite was a star of such magnitude that, during a portion of our interview conducted in a public congressional chamber, a woman tourist rushed past a tall, handsome senator to ask for Sandman's autograph. The senator was Edward Kennedy.

That afternoon I returned to Philadelphia and banged out the story on my typewriter. It was the kind of story reporters dream about; Sandman was so colorful and quotable that it practically wrote itself. It began:

WASHINGTON—An aide to Rep. Charles W. Sandman Jr. leans back into the studded, black leather chair, dangles his left leg over the mahogany armrest and speaks loudly into the aqua-colored telephone.

"Well, Congressman Sandman has Mike Douglas hanging now and he's very tired," he tells the television network booking agent at the other end of the line.

"I can't give you a definite answer right now. But let me just say, between you and me, that I'm damned sure he'll do it."

At the end of a week's worth of live television coverage of the House Judiciary Committee hearings, Charles Sandman, son of a South Jersey milk deliveryman, has suddenly become the hottest instant celebrity since Tiny Tim.

Douglas wants the paunchy, 52-year-old congressman for an appearance with Martha Mitchell. A T-shirt firm wants to emblazon Sandman's craggy face across the chest of millions. ABC television is planning a mini-documentary on his life.

Sandman has even become the celebrity most other celebrities talk about on talk shows. "He comes off like a classic villain," Orson Bean said last week on "The Johnny Carson Show."

Not to everyone, Orson, not to everyone.

Just as Sam Ervin, the folksy country lawyer from North Carolina, became the folk hero of millions of anti-Nixonites during last year's Senate Watergate hearings, Sandman, the feisty ex-boxer from Cape May, N. J., attained similar instant status among pro-Nixonites during the House Judiciary Committee hearings

The article continued to describe Sandman's obvious glee at his newfound notoriety. He even confessed at one point that he was now entertaining vice-presidential aspirations.

Unhappily for Sandman, the President announced his resignation just as the congressman was getting into high gear. In the blizzard of coverage about Nixon, Sandman was quickly forgotten by *The Mike Douglas Show*, the T-shirt company, and ABC. Farewell, instant celebrity.

My last Watergate story occurred on the night Nixon appeared on coast-to-coast television to announce that he was leaving office. At that time, August 8, 1974, several of his aides already were serving prison terms in connection with the administration scandal. One of them, Jeb Magruder, was fulfilling his sentence at Allenwood Federal Prison, located about 150 miles from Philadelphia.

Although Nixon didn't announce his resignation until late in the day, it was no secret for hours beforehand. Typically, one of the White House aides had leaked word of the impending development.

"Say, Kathy, why don't you go up to Allenwood and watch Nixon's press conference with Jeb Magruder?" one of the editors suggested. "His reaction might be very interesting."

I'm sure that it was. Too bad I never got to see it.

When I got to Allenwood, a four-thousand-acre camp regarded as the country club of the federal prison system, the warden was quite cooperative about my request to watch television with Magruder. Unfortunately, the prisoners weren't. Evidently the only available televisions were all located in the community rooms of the prison's eight fifty-bed dormitories. And the prisoners didn't want a woman sitting in their midst.

"The men usually wear their skivvies while watching

TV," the warden explained a bit sheepishly. "And I'm afraid they wouldn't appreciate your presence."

Although I momentarily was tempted to offer to get in my skivvies too, I realized that it probably wouldn't help. I sensed that Magruder didn't want to be interviewed anyway. I was right.

When it became obvious that I was not going to be able to talk directly to Magruder, I decided to interview some of the prisoners who were wandering around, fully dressed, in the administration section of the prison. As a reporter, I long ago had learned that I could not always obtain the exact story originally conceived by an editor. But I could always obtain some story.

In this case, the inmates had some interesting perceptions on Nixon's legal status.

"We've got a nice bed ready for Nixon," said one bank robber. "But I doubt that he'll ever come here. He'll get out of it."

9--Mass Murders

The date on my 1975 calendar was circled in red: Friday, March 28. It was my twenty-seventh birthday, and Wiley and I were planning to have a special celebration. We had reservations for dinner at Le Bec Fin, generally acknowledged as the finest—and most expensive—restaurant in Philadelphia. Tonight was going to be magnificent.

Because Le Bec Fin has only two dinner seatings per evening, at 6 and 9 P.M., we had chosen the later hour. That would give me plenty of time to go home after work and change into my fancy clothes. Or so I thought.

About 5 P.M., I was sitting at my desk daydreaming about the sumptuous evening ahead: wine, candlelight, impeccable service. As I was deciding whether I would order quenelles or pâté as an appetizer, my reverie abruptly was ended by a shout from one of my editors.

"We just got a call that there's a sniper loose in Mount Holly," he said. "Kathy, take a company car and get over there immediately."

In the hubbub I grabbed the phone to call Wiley, who was going to pick me up after work. Uh-oh, no answer;

114

too late. Wiley probably was already on his way to the *Inquirer*. I scrawled out a cryptic note and left it on my typewriter. "Had to go to Mount Holly. Sniper shooting at police. Will call you at home."

As I drove to Mount Holly, a New Jersey suburb located about twenty-five miles outside Philadelphia, I figured the wisest course would be to go directly to the police station to determine if the sniper tip was true.

It was. When I got to headquarters, the police said that the gunman was holed up in a house on Garden Street and was shooting from an upper-story window. Two policemen already had been killed.

"That's all the information we have right now," a police dispatcher said. "The phones haven't stopped ringing since this happened."

Because I obviously wasn't going to get a firsthand story at the police station, I got in my car and drove over to Garden Street. It was a spine-tingling sight. The normally quiet, tree-lined street looked like the setting for a modern disaster movie: floodlights, police cars, and firetrucks were everywhere. As local officials used bullhorns to try to persuade the sniper to give himself up, hundreds of neighbors milled behind the barricades cordoning off the area outside the gunman's hideout.

"Wow, this is the most exciting thing that's ever happened in Mount Holly," one fifteen-year-old boy said.

For the first hour after my arrival, everyone was tensely awaiting the next burst of gunfire. It didn't come. So, almost like a circus audience breathlessly waiting for the daring aerialist to fall from the tightrope, the neighbors began speculating about the identity of the sniper and making bets about his next move.

"I heard the guy's a Vietnam veteran," said one woman.

"Yeah, a real loner," added another.

"I think his girlfriend just broke up with him," said a third spectator.

At about 8 P.M. I called the office to tell the editors what was happening. They told me to "stay with it."

"By the way, did Wiley come in the office?" I asked.

"Yeah, but he already left," the editor said.

I made a quick call to Wiley at home. Again, no answer. I checked my watch: 8:30 P.M. I wondered if he was having my birthday celebration without me.

Shortly after 10 P.M. about a dozen policemen stormed the three-story white frame house where the sniper was hiding. After throwing several tear-gas canisters into the building, the uniformed men riddled the door of a bedroom with bullets and then forced it open.

The sniper, bleeding from a gunshot wound in the buttocks, was huddled in a corner of the room. The police wrapped him in a blanket and carried him out.

I hurried back to the police station to obtain some background information on the suspect. Then I called the *Inquirer*. I noted with satisfaction that it was still early enough to get the story into the final edition.

"Great, great," the editor said. "But we'll need a lot more information for a big Sunday story. Can you stick around and get as much background as possible on the two dead policemen and everyone else involved?"

I groaned. Some birthday celebration this had turned out to be. But I knew the *Inquirer* was relying on me.

"I'll do the best I can," I said.

As I was hanging up the phone, I noticed that a wall clock nearby said 11:50 P.M. Only ten minutes left of my birthday. But all was not completely lost, for suddenly Wiley rushed into the police station.

"Thank God, you're safe!" He was not quite his usual

cool self. "I couldn't wait at home any longer. I kept thinking about all the stories I've read about people being killed in horrible accidents on their birthdays—or anniversaries—and I got really worried about you."

Sadly enough, one of the slain policeman did die on his birthday. Like me, he had been planning a big celebration before he was called in to work that night. I shuddered when I saw his wife arrive at the station in evening dress.

At 1:30 A.M. the police chief announced that he would hold a press conference within the next few minutes. The next few minutes somehow stretched into an hour. Wiley and I and the rest of the reporters tried to make ourselves comfortable on the hallway steps.

"Happy birthday to me, a happy birthday to me," I chanted.

By 3:30 A.M. I had filled two notebooks with information on both the suspect and the victims. I was ready to call it a night.

"Go home," the editor said when I called in. "We'll see you tomorrow."

Wearily Wiley and I headed for our cars. In all the excitement, I had forgotten that I hadn't eaten dinner yet. Neither had Wiley.

"Do you think that Le Bec Fin kept our meal warm for us?" I joked.

As it turned out, we wound up grabbing a bite to eat at a nearby diner. My hamburger didn't taste as good as Beef Wellington, but I knew I would be able to have my birthday dinner some other time. I wished the slain policeman had been as lucky.

Almost a year later, there was another highly publicized murder case in the Philadelphia area. Five members of the John Abt family and a family friend were found shot to death in their home in Trevose, located just outside the city border. This time I heard about the senseless crime on my car radio. It was my day off, and I was glad.

"I'd hate to have to talk to the survivors of this one," I said to a friend.

I spoke too soon.

Because the murder had been so heinous, the *Inquirer* editors decided to assign a team of reporters to investigate the crime, which still was unsolved three days later. I was part of the team.

Although the murders had been discovered on Friday, none of the city papers had yet contacted the obvious interviewee: the Abts' twenty-year-old son, Michael, who had discovered the bodies. Much as I hated the idea of approaching someone so emotionally involved, I felt that the young man might provide the key to the puzzling slayings. I volunteered to try and find him.

"Okay, but be careful," said my editor, Max, who was directing the team effort. "We really don't know if Michael is a suspect or not."

As it happened, I never got the chance to try to talk Michael Abt into an interview. On the day of my attempt, he had gone into seclusion with relatives. And no one would say where he was.

As I was trying to locate Michael, I spoke at length with a young man who said he lived on the same block. He said he truly was sorry about his neighbors' deaths because they were a nice family and they never bothered anybody. Because the comments were so innocuous, I didn't even bother to get the young man's name. He clearly wasn't worth a story.

A few days later, the *Inquirer* sent me to cover the Abts'

funeral. Because a suspect still had not been found, the church was crowded with policemen anxiously watching the crowd. There was some fear that the killer might show up and shoot Michael and his only other surviving brother, Clifford.

Fortunately, there was no incident at the funeral. I probably was responsible for the single biggest disruption when I tried to interview a teenage girl who was sobbing in the back of the church. She could not bear to look at the six caskets lined up single file in the church aisle.

"I was the best friend Kathy [Abt] ever had!" the girl cried. "I just can't believe this could happen."

As I engaged the girl in conversation, an older man walked over, his fists clenched tightly at his sides.

"Are you a reporter?" he asked.

"Yes," I replied.

"Then get away from this girl or I'm going to punch you in the mouth."

I can't say that I blamed him.

A few days after the funeral the police announced that they had taken a young man in his early twenties into custody. A neighbor, the suspect apparently had a long-standing grudge against the Abt family.

When I saw the man's photograph, I was totally shocked. He was the same person I had spoken to the day I was looking for Michael Abt. So much for my news judgment!

On another occasion I unwittingly had spent some time with a man who eventually would be accused of murder. Then, however, I believe I came a lot closer to becoming a victim.

In March 1974 I was assigned to do a story on a man

who just had been released from jail after his son testified that he had lied during his earlier trial on charges of child beating. The idea of the article was to focus on the reaction of a father whose son caused him to serve seven months in prison.

"Wow, if I didn't beat the kid before, I think I would if he pulled something like that on me," I said when I heard about the case.

Much to my surprise, however, the man, whose name was Joseph Kallinger, expressed no animosity or bitterness toward his son. In soft tones Kallinger explained to me that his son hadn't realized what he was doing, hadn't meant to send his father to jail, hadn't considered the consequences of his lies.

I thought Kallinger was either a saint or completely nuts. The latter turned out to be closer to the truth.

A few days after the interview, Kallinger called me to say that his son had run away from home.

"Can you come over and help me?" he asked.

I said I was busy, but perhaps the *Inquirer* could send another reporter. He said to forget about it.

About a week later Kallinger called again to invite me to visit his shoe-repair shop. I declined.

A month after that, he made a third call to tell me that his son was having problems with the police. He wanted to get the story into the paper. I said the *Inquirer* probably wouldn't be interested.

After that, Kallinger stopped calling. The next thing I read about him was that his son had been found dead at the bottom of a rock pile. The death was ruled accidental.

A few months after that, the Philadelphia papers were bursting with stories about an epidemic of rapes in North Jersey. The assailants all fit the same description. At the height of the spree of sexual attacks, one nurse from Leonia fiercely resisted the rapist. She was killed.

As I read about the incidents, I was appalled at the violence and viciousness exhibited by the attacker. I was even more appalled when Kallinger was arrested as the suspect in the long series of assaults against women.

"Wow, he may not even be guilty!" I told a friend. "But I sure am glad I never saw him again after that first interview."

While most people seem to have a certain amount of morbid curiosity about the grisly physical details of a murder, I seem to have a strange fascination for the emotional aftermath of crime. Whenever I read about a homicide, I never think about the immediate questions: Where was the body found? What was the weapon used? Who are the suspects? Instead, I tend to wonder about the long-range effects on the survivors, the neighbors, even the buildings.

Early in 1974 I read a brief news story about the Clutter farm in Garden City, Kansas, the central scene of Truman Capote's well-known book *In Cold Blood*. The article noted that the farmhouse where the four Clutters were killed had been for sale for more than a year, but no one wanted to buy it.

The Clutter story sparked an idea in my mind to see what had happened to several buildings in the Philadelphia area that also had been the scenes of shocking crimes. Like most journalists, I viewed this not as stealing but as extending the original article. (A surprising number of newspaper and magazine stories are offshoots of earlier pieces in another publication.)

The idea turned out to be a good one. The buildings almost breathed with their histories. An office complex in Cherry Hill, New Jersey, where six persons had been shot to death by a crazed gunman practically was vacant two years after the crime. All of the former tenants moved out. A barber shop in Camden, New Jersey, which had been connected with the mass murder of thirteen innocent persons dropped in value to less than half its original cost. A private home in suburban Philadelphia where a man had killed most of his family before turning the gun on himself was sold far below the average market price in the neighborhood.

I began the story like this:

Nestled behind a group of fir trees, the two-story Colonial house at 639 Twickenham Drive looks like every family's dream—freshly painted, spacious, conveniently situated.

Yet when this dream house in Glenside went up for sale three years ago, at a bargain price of $45,000 in a $60,000 neighborhood, it took the realtor almost a year to find a buyer.

Why? The previous owner was a 42-year-old Montgomery County businessman who shot to death his wife and four of his five children and then ended his own life in the home.

"When we told people we were going to move in there, they said we were nuts," said the new owner. "But what difference does it make?"

As intriguing as I found the topic of blood-soaked properties, I had to admit that I admired the family's reasonable outlook. I don't think I would have had the nerve to move into the house. Chalk one up for superstition.

10--Celebrities

Donald Sutherland and Elliott Gould ambled into the hotel room and settled their lean, angular bodies into the high-backed, brocaded chairs directly across from me. Sutherland, wearing a wide-brimmed white hat, stared at me expectantly. Gould stuffed a piece of bubble gum into his mouth.

Without a doubt I was in a position most women would envy: sitting in a hotel room with not one, but two, of the most famous movie stars in the country. I realized that many people, for a chance to be in my seat, would have sacrificed a lot.

Yet I didn't want to be there.

To most people, one of the most glamorous aspects of being a reporter is the opportunity to hobnob with celebrities. During my career the questions I frequently was asked were whether I had ever met so-and-so and what was he really like.

The general public does not realize that most reporters, with the exception of movie-star "specialists" such as Rex Reed or Rona Barrett, rarely get a chance to talk with celebrities about their personal feelings or beliefs. Ninety-nine percent of the interviews are scheduled so that the movie star can push his or her latest movie or TV show or book.

On the day of my interview with Sutherland and Gould, they were in the midst of a week-long promotional tour for their new film entitled *S*P*Y*S*. Both were tired, edgy, and bored. They had good reason.

When I showed up in their hotel suite for what I thought was going to be an exclusive interview, I found a dozen other reporters already waiting for the arrival of the two stars. I sensed immediately that the situation was going to be disastrous. It was.

When Sutherland and Gould showed up, the reporters began asking for information that easily could be found in any newspaper library: What was their last picture? How did Sutherland get his start? How long was Gould married to Barbra Streisand?

The questions were so trivial that I was embarrassed. Sutherland did his best to remain attentive. Gould didn't even try. In the middle of the press conference he turned on the television and started watching an afternoon game show.

At the end of the session, as the other reporters filed out of the suite, I asked Sutherland how he could stand being asked such stupid questions by reporters who obviously hadn't done their homework. He shrugged.

When I wrote the story later that afternoon, I tried to capture the mood of the entire session. The story began:

It was hard to figure out the object of the game.

Elliott Gould didn't seem to understand the rules at all. Donald Sutherland was doing his best to determine them, but he was continually distracted by questions from reporters.

Dick Clark was no help either. Although Clark was the host of the game show being aired on the television in a corner of the hotel suite, he never bothered to explain how to play.

Clue words kept flashing onto the screen and Elliott Gould just kept repeating them.

"Yo hum," 35-year-old Gould said between loud chomps on the pink bubblegum evident between his teeth.

"That's a joke," Sutherland, 39, explained, pointing almost apologetically to the "Yo-Hum" flashed across the screen.

The game was being played during a press conference in the stars' suite at the Bellevue Stratford, arranged as a promotion for a new film called S*P*Y*S pairing Gould and Sutherland as CIA agents similar to the characters that made M*A*S*H such a S*M*A*S*H.

Twentieth Century-Fox was anxious to prove that some bad New York reviews of S*P*Y*S, now playing at the Eric's Mark I, were all L*I*E*S.

Neither Gould nor Sutherland seemed particularly excited about being in Philadelphia as part of their week-long, seven-interviews-per-day promotional tour, but then it was all part of the, er, business.

"It's part of the whole process of filmmaking," Sutherland said, lifting the legs of his 6-foot-4-inch frame onto the Chippendale coffee table. "If you want to fully participate, you have to be interested in the way a film is sold and distributed."

Sutherland turned slightly in his flowered, high-backed chair to give Gould an opportunity to express himself.

"Huh?" Gould said as the eyes of a group of reporters turned to meet his eyes, which were still staring intently at the TV screen. "What? Huh?"

Not all celebrity interviews take place in hotel rooms. In Philadelphia the majority probably take place in the dressing rooms of the televised *Mike Douglas Show*.

At the beginning of each week the Douglas staff mails to the area newspapers a list of all the guests that will be appearing within the next few days. They also carefully note which celebrities will be available for interviews.

The system works nicely for all concerned. The stars like it because it gives them an opportunity to plug their latest movies. Mike Douglas likes it because his show is invariably mentioned in every story. The editors like it because it provides them with enough articles to fill the Sunday entertainment pages.

I hated it. Why? Because I think interviews conducted this way usually are stiff and artificial.

The first time I went to the Douglas studio near Independence Hall in Philadelphia was to talk to the Smothers Brothers about one of their many comebacks. An avid fan of the noncomformist comedians, I fully expected to spend an hour or so doubled over in laughter at their wit and antics. Was I ever surprised!

When I arrived, a Douglas aide informed me that my interview, which was to be sandwiched between sessions with reporters from the Philadelphia *Bulletin* and the Philadelphia *Daily News*, must be limited to fifteen minutes. Although I was disappointed at the time rule, I was relieved to know that my conversation with the two comedians at least was going to be private. Wrong again.

When I met the Smotherses in their dressing room, they were accompanied by their publicity manager, who obviously had no intentions of leaving. I had learned long ago that the main function of a press aide is to steer every conversation away from personal matters and veer it back to commercial ventures. This guy was no exception.

The interview was one of the dullest I ever have had. Instead of cracking jokes, Dickie Smothers spent most of the time complaining about the dust in the dressing room. Tommy Smothers' main topic of conversation was the smoke curling from his eight-inch cigar. Dickie made only one attempt at humor, when he discussed his reasons for remarrying the same wife he had divorced a year or so before.

"I didn't have much choice. She had all of my money and all of my children," he said. "I actually married a very wealthy divorcee with three kids."

After my fifteen minutes were up, I decided that the only way to salvage my story was to stick around the set for a while. One of the basic tricks of interviewing is to remain with a subject after he or she has run out of prepared remarks. That's when they usually begin babbling on to avoid gaps in the conversation and, in the process, start revealing their most intimate secrets.

After completing their other interviews, the Smotherses began taping the show. They were scheduled to appear right after country-music singer Loretta Lynn, the show's cohostess of the week. The brothers sang a song and then sat down for a few minutes of snappy patter with Douglas, who followed his usual practice of reading all of his questions from cue cards.

During a routine commercial break, Tommy and

Dickie were recycled to other chairs to make room for Broadway comedian Carol Channing, whose mammoth eyes looked as if they had been framed with every false eyelash from the makeup department's sizable collection.

Following a song from her show, *Lorelei*, Miss Channing walked over to the conversation area and pressed her blood-red lips against Douglas' cheek. Next she kissed Loretta Lynn. Dick Smothers was next in line. He drew back slightly as Miss Channing approached. She settled for a handshake.

In the makeup room after the show, Dick Smothers admitted that it was somewhat disconcerting to appear on a show with entertainers "out of our spectrum." Especially when they tried to kiss him.

"But," Smothers said as he wiped off his makeup with Sea Breeze astringent, "in a case like this, you have to just sit there. You can't just eat and run, after all."

Despite my dislike for interviewing celebrities about their next project, I must admit that I truly marvel at their energy. I suspect that some movie stars talk in their sleep about how wonderful their next movie is, how clever their latest TV show will be, how spectacularly their new book is selling.

One night I attended a cast party for a play that featured Robert Stack and Joanne Pflug. Although the affair wasn't set up as a press event, Stack talked on and on about the new direction his career was taking.

"I'd like to get into comedy," Stack said. "Or to work in almost any part with a top director like Mike Nichols."

What Stack wanted most, he said, was to get away from his Elliott Ness image from the old TV show *The Untouchables*.

"I think I'll be successful," Stack said as he passed up a calorie-laden plate of cold cuts and potato salad in favor of a slice of watermelon.

He spoke too soon. As Stack was finishing his fruit, a jovial middle-aged woman came up and grabbed his arm.

"I watch reruns of *The Untouchables* all the time," the woman said. "I can't imagine you in any other role."

Of course, Robert Stack is hardly the only celebrity with an image problem. Take Dick Clark. Although Clark became a successful producer, businessman, and game-show host, most people associate him most closely with *American Bandstand*.

In 1975 I was sent to cover the taping of a *Bandstand* special at its old studio in West Philadelphia. Clark had invited all of the show's "regulars" from the late 1950s to participate in the taping. Once again I was amazed at the difference between a celebrity's public image and his private personality.

As a child I always had perceived Clark as the eternally cheerful host of the dance show. On the night of the taping, he was anything but cheerful. It was late, after all, and the production was taking a lot longer than he had expected. He became curt.

When I wrote the story, I tried to contrast the past and present images of both Clark and the "regulars." Several of the former teenage ministars called later to complain that I had made them look foolish in my article. I disagreed. If they looked foolish, and I didn't think anyone had, it was their own fault. I only wrote what I saw. And here are some of my observations:

Back in the heyday of American Bandstand, when Arlene Sullivan and Kenny Rossi were as well known to U.S. teenagers as Lucille Ball and Desi Arnaz were to their parents, Dick Clark laid down a series of on-camera rules for the program's "regulars":

No drinking. No smoking. No slacks. No tight sweaters. No gum chewing.

How times have changed.

About a half hour before the taping of segments of a 90-minute Bandstand special which will be on channel 6 at 11:30 p.m. May 9, Eliott Jurist, 30, of Caribe Caterers, was busy opening three cases of champagne for the televised party.

And the old regulars, some of whom now, oddly enough, look older at age 30 than Clark does at age 45, were getting into the spirit of things.

Monty Montez, 30, a teacher's aide in Camden, was busy sipping champagne as other old regulars heaped their plates full of chopped liver, shrimp and melon balls from a nearby buffet table.

Montez, whose memory of winning fourth place in Bandstand's 1962 mashed potatoes dance contest is matched only by being on the all-Camden basketball team in high school, was recalling how he got to be a dancer on the show.

"I used to fight to get in front of the line," he said with a grin.

Of all the celebrities I've interviewed, a group which also includes comedians Anne Meara and Jerry Stiller, Mrs. Eunice Kennedy Shriver, and others, my favorite was Burt Mustin.

Burt who?

Although Mustin had been a frequent guest on the *Johnny Carson Show* and then appeared regularly on the *Phyllis Show* before his death in January, 1977, his name still was largely unknown among the general public. But nearly everyone knew his face.

"A lot of people identify me with somebody they know, but they just can't place me," Mustin said when I interviewed him back in 1967.

Although Mustin was working regularly at that time, he seemed almost reluctant to plug his various roles. I practically had to pry out of the kindly actor, who was then eighty-three years old, that he had been cast as Tarzan in an upcoming TV comedy.

Mustin wanted mostly to talk about his wife, whom he had married more than fifty years before.

"When I was at military school, my wife's picture was hanging up on the wall in a friend's room," Mustin said.

"My friend was a real ladies' man and we fellows greatly admired him because he had such a lovely group on his wall. Well, I eventually married one of them—the loveliest of all."

For all my criticism about interviewing celebrities, I can sympathize with their frequent reluctance to open up to the press. For one thing, many famous people unjustly have been maligned and criticized by newspaper reporters. And for another, most celebrities, because of the public nature of their work, have a difficult time maintaining any privacy.

I had a brief taste of celebrity status in 1973 when the *Inquirer* asked me to do a weekly woman-around-town column entitled "On the Go." My duties included eating at local restaurants, drinking at local bars, and reviewing local shows—all on the newspaper's money. It sounded like a dream. But it quickly turned into a nightmare.

After "On the Go," accompanied by my photograph, had been running for a few weeks, I started to be recognized everywhere I went. At first I was completely surprised because I never had obtained such mass recognition from my earlier columns at the *Daily Times* and the *Courier-Post*. But I had forgotten one important fact: the *Inquirer* had four times as many readers as my former papers combined.

Initially I was flattered when restaurant owners and local "beautiful people" recognized me. But the thrill quickly died out. More often than not, I found myself in the awkward position of being offered free meals, free drinks, free entertainment. Much as I objected, no one wanted to accept payment from my expense account. The unspoken assumption was that I would repay everyone with a mention in my column.

I did not like being bought off.

Even with people on the street the situation got out of hand. I was recognized in train stations, laundromats, even in ladies' rooms. Fame was getting downright embarrassing.

About a month after the column began I actually perceived a change in my personality. I was afraid to step outside my door unless my hair was curled, my clothes clean, my makeup perfect. I even became reluctant to wear blue jeans.

"Wow, this is ridiculous," I said to myself one Saturday morning when I found myself getting all dressed up to go buy a quart of milk. "I'm going out in my T-shirt and shorts."

Unfortunately, one of my readers was shopping at the same market. As I reached in the dairy case, I noticed her staring at my un-madeup face. Then she spoke to me, "Wow, you're Kathy Begley, aren't you?"

I glumly assented.

"Boy, you don't look anything like your picture—I thought you were a lot prettier."

That did it. I resigned from the column the following Monday.

11--Teaching

One by one, the students began filing into the classroom at Temple University's suburban campus in Ambler, Pennsylvania. One, a man in his early forties, asked why I had decided to take the course.

"I guess because I'm the teacher," I said.

"You're kidding," he said, peering at my twenty-five-year-old face. "You look like you're in high school."

It was 1973 and I had agreed to teach my first newswriting course at Temple, which had one of the most comprehensive journalism programs in Pennsylvania. Like many reporters in midcareer, I felt I needed some feedback, and I hoped I would get plenty in the college classroom. I was right. Maybe my students taught me more than I did them.

As a working reporter, I tried hard to make my course as practical as possible. I think education should be every bit as concerned with giving students marketable skills as philosophical thoughts. Writing poetry is a noble pursuit, but it's usually not very profitable.

Consequently I tried to teach my students the essentials of everyday newswriting: how to conduct a successful interview; how to research a particular topic; how to write a story in "inverted pyramid" style, which means arranging the facts in the order of their importance. In turn, the students taught me how fulfilling a classroom experience can be.

"This is the most enjoyable class I've ever had," one student told me at the end of the semester.

Not everyone felt that way, however. A few weeks after the term began, I noticed that one of my pupils had stopped attending classes. I assumed he had dropped the course. Then, about two weeks before finals, he suddenly reappeared and said he would like to get credit and take the examination. I was skeptical.

"I don't think it would be fair to yourself or to the other students," I said. "After all, you've been to only one or two classes."

"But I have a good excuse," he said.

"Oh?" I asked.

"Yeah, yeah, I've been in jail for over a month."

When I looked quizzical, the student proudly pulled a newspaper clipping out of the pocket of his leather jacket. There, in inverted pyramid style, was the story of his arrest for possession of drugs.

"Well," I said, "I have to admit that it's more original than a doctor's note."

As it turned out, I gave the student permission to take the final, but he never showed up. He phoned me that he had been arrested again. When it came time to fill out my grade cards, I decided to give him a "W" for withdrawal rather than an "F" for failure. I figured he had enough problems.

During the next three years I taught four more courses at three Philadelphia colleges—Temple, Community

College, and St. Joseph's. As in my first class, I always tried to make learning as practical and enjoyable as possible. The students, as I wanted, always tried to make teaching as demanding and challenging as possible.

As in any occupation, newspaper work requires a certain amount of skills that you rarely read about in textbooks. There are many little tricks or shortcuts that make a reporter's job much easier. I frequently tried to impart some of these aids to my students.

One of my favorite tips to students was what I called the "Little Notebook Theory." To illustrate what I meant, I frequently told them this story.

Once, while I was working at the *Courier-Post*, I was sent to interview a woman who had won close to one million dollars in the New Jersey State Lottery. The woman, a fifty-year-old housewife, never had been interviewed before and almost was shaking with fear. She practically fainted when I took my notebook, which measured about five by seven inches, out of my pocketbook.

"My God, what's that?" she gasped. "You're not going to write down everything I say?"

"Only a few things," I said. "I mean, you did agree to the story."

"Oh, yes, yes, I know," she said. "But I don't speak too good and that notebook makes me scared."

Taking the hint, I stuffed the pad back into my purse. Instead of taking notes, I carefully memorized a few key phrases used by the interviewee. Once, I even asked to use the bathroom so I could scribble down a few quotes before I forgot them.

When the article appeared in the newspaper, the woman called to tell me she had loved it. She apologized profusely for being so nervous. I didn't mind because the experience had taught me a good lesson. When dealing with inexperienced subjects, I never again used a large, threatening notebook.

Like most theories, of course, mine has a converse rule. I call that the "Big Notebook Theory." In my discussions about this, I usually told my students about another incident.

When I first started working at the *Daily Times*, I was assigned for a short time to the police beat. As part of my duties I was required to drive each day to the hospital and to the police station to read all the accident and crime reports. The biggest problem was that the reports usually were incomplete or inaccurate. Therefore, I often had to seek out nurses or policemen to obtain further information.

One day I needed more facts on a robbery story. I walked hesitantly into the office of a detective who had a reputation for disliking reporters. Gulping, I asked him for the details I needed.

"I really need this information," I said. "But I guess you don't want to tell me, do you?"

The detective looked at me in disbelief. Then he started laughing.

"Look, kid, I don't think anyone is ever going to believe you're a reporter," he said. "What you need is a giant notebook."

From that day on, whenever I was sent to interview important businessmen or legal authorities, I took a large notebook. I'm not sure that it ever made them any more confident of my abilities, but it certainly helped me. Perhaps I should rename this the Security Blanket Theory.

Of all the incidents I used to tell my students, my favorite concerned a time when I dressed as a nurse in order to interview a young boy who had been shot by police during riots in Camden, New Jersey, in 1971. I used the story to illustrate the occasional necessity of using unorthodox means to obtain a story. Because of the nature of the particular case, I felt that I was entirely justified in misrepresenting myself at the hospital. I firmly believed, and still do, that my actions were ethical because I used deceit only to gain access to the interviewee. I did not use deceit to get the interviewee to talk with me.

Many of my students disagreed.

"Didn't you feel bad disrupting the hospital rules?" one woman asked. "What about all those other sick people?

"And how about the kid?" added another student. "How could you interview him without his parents' permission?"

"Let's face it," said a third person. "You lied. How can you ever rationalize that?"

So much for feedback.

Another technique I employed frequently in the classroom was to stage mock press conferences and events. Once, pretending to be the White House press secretary, I announced that Betty Ford was running off with Steve McQueen. Another time, acting as Elizabeth Taylor's publicity woman, I publicized the actress' purchase of the Empire State Building.

But my most memorable staged event was the time I posed as Bella Abzug. A week beforehand, I had instructed my students to come to class prepared to ask questions as if they were attending a real press conference. Afterward, they would write the story for "deadline" and hand it in to me.

Before driving to class, I wrote a lengthy speech,

calling for passage of the Equal Rights Amendment, election of more women legislators, and consumer pressures on discriminating employers and industries. I got so carried away that I didn't leave my apartment until the last minute.

When I got to Temple's suburban campus, I figured I'd cut across a big field to save some time. I didn't realize until I was halfway across that the ground was mushy and soggy from several days of rain. As I was considering whether or not to turn back, my feet suddenly slipped out from under me. I fell facedown in the mud.

When I entered the classroom, looking quite similar to Pigpen in the Peanuts cartoon strip, I deliberately didn't explain what had happened. I launched immediately into my Bella Abzug speech.

During the question-and-answer period afterward, a student asked what had happened. Still pretending to be Ms. Abzug, I said that a group of anti-feminists had dragged me from my limousine, spat on me, and pushed me into a mud puddle.

Apparently I was not altogether convincing. When I read the stories later that night, only two of fifteen students mentioned the mud fight in the lead of their articles. If the incident had been true, it definitely would have been page-one news all over the country. All of which goes to show, I suppose, that teachers never can fully simulate real life in the classroom. But I still think it's valuable to try.

The one truly unpleasant aspect of teaching was my inside knowledge of the opportunities available in today's journalism job market. There simply aren't that many.

As recently as 1966, when I obtained my first job, newspapers were largely a seller's market. Good reporters could sell themselves anywhere in a profession that was not yet considered particularly attractive or glamorous.

But all of that has changed in recent years. With the development of "star" reporters such as Washington *Post* writer Sally Quinn, journalism has become THE profession. All over the country, colleges and universities are churning out more and more graduates of mass-communications curricula. But, unfortunately, no one is churning out more jobs. Consequently, thousands of aspiring journalists are unemployed.

Translated into the classroom, the depressing state of the job market always made it difficult for me to offer solid, concrete advice to students interested in pursuing journalism as a professional career. But I tried to be as encouraging yet realistic as I could.

On the first day of every course, my students inevitably asked me how I got my start. They always found the story of my car accident very entertaining but hardly practical. Unfortunately, I agreed.

"I mean, let's face it, I wouldn't recommend your cracking up your car." I would laugh.

The most practical advice I could give was to start small. For some reason, many journalism graduates expect to begin their careers at the New York *Times*. I know of only one person who did—and he started as a copyboy, not a reporter. For the most part the only writers who start at the top are the ones who know somebody at the top.

"But you can't let that get you down—the old line that you have to know somebody," I often told my students. "You have to make yourself known."

And the best way, in my opinion, is to take a job on a small weekly paper so that a reporter can obtain both experience and, most importantly, published writing to show on the next job interview. My advice is nothing new; it's journalism's version of the big-fish-in-the-small-pond theory. But I honestly believe it works.

It did for me.

12--The End

Thomas J. Hamilton pulled his sled up to the edge of his garden, inserted his arm into a hole, and then dug a little deeper until his shoulder was at ground level.

"That's how I can tell the hole is deep enough for the fence," Hamilton said as he inserted a white picket into the dirt.

I watched in open-mouthed amazement, not because making a picket fence is an extraordinary achievement but because Hamilton clearly was an extraordinary man. He had recently had both of his legs amputated and he had gone totally blind.

At the time I interviewed him in the summer of 1967, Hamilton was being honored by the local American Legion Post for a variety of volunteer and charitable work. Hamilton just had turned seventy-two. I just had turned nineteen. I fell in love with him immediately.

"I've lost my legs, my hair, my teeth, and my sight—but not my faith," Hamilton said as he groped back to his house to introduce me to his wife, who had helped him through his diabetes-related amputations and blindness.

"No matter whatever happens," Hamilton said, "we must always remember that tomorrow is a better day."

As I drove back to the city room, I thought of the bittersweet character of the man. Hamilton touched me as no one before with his inner warmth, compassion, and generosity. When I mentioned my feelings back at the office, one of the other reporters laughed.

"Ah, just another sob story," he said.

But I didn't care. Not then. I wrote a story that drew almost a hundred letters responding to the decency and strength of Thomas Hamilton.

Like any business, journalism tends to pigeonhole people. If you write a particular kind of story well once, you'll probably be assigned to write fifty more. Because I am basically a sensitive person, I often was given stories that editors regarded as sensitive subjects. My problem was that I often did not agree on their definition of "sensitive." Neither did many of the other reporters.

"Wow, if I had to write all the tearjerkers like you do, I think I'd quit," a fellow *Daily Times* reporter once told me. "You're a real sob sister."

In this journalistic age, being called a sob sister is the worse thing imaginable. Tell a reporter they're gutsy like Jack Anderson; or boring like William Buckley; or bitchy like Suzy Knickerbocker. But never tell them they're a sob sister.

As the years went by, I learned to defend myself against such an image. Although I never refused an assignment concerning sadness and misfortune, I often scoffed and joked at the subject matter on my way out of the city-room door. Clearly, I was destined for greater things: war, pestilence, and plague. And maybe a flood or two.

By the spring of 1976, when I had been a professional

journalist for ten long years, I had learned the game well. Usually I was able to pick and choose my assignments. And I rarely picked or chose a tearjerker.

However, one morning I read a story that had an unusual twist. A woman in northeast Philadelphia had had her finger bitten off by a police horse. I decided to interview her on a hunch that the story might lend itself to a light, humorous treatment. It did.

When the article appeared the following day, the victim called to tell me she loved the story. So, unfortunately, did the editors.

That afternoon, Jerry Mondesire, one of the *Inquirer*'s day editors, came over to my desk. He told me he had loved the story on the fingerless woman and now had a similar assignment for me. He asked if I would like to go interview a handless woman and her blind husband, who had just won several thousand dollars in the Pennsylvania lottery.

"You've got to be kidding," I said with a groan.

"No, no, it's a good story," Jerry said.

"Okay, so get someone else to do it," I said.

A few minutes later I felt guilty that I had all but refused to do the assignment. Jerry, after all, had just started work as an editor after spending several years as a reporter. I knew the assignment probably wasn't his idea, and I didn't want to cause him any unnecessary problems.

"Okay, I'll do it," I said. "But I still think it's a lousy story."

When I got to the couple's home, I worked more than usual in obtaining a good interview. Whenever I thought a story idea was bad, I always tried doubly hard to salvage it. Sometimes it worked, sometimes it didn't. In this case the interview came out okay.

The woman, as it turned out, had been born without hands due to a birth defect. Her husband had been blind since infancy. Before winning the lottery, their only other stroke of luck had been in meeting each other.

"See, that story wasn't so bad," Jerry told me the day the article appeared. "And you pooh-poohed it."

If the matter had died there, I probably would have forgotten about it. But an hour later Max King, who had read the fingerless and handless stories but didn't know my feelings about them, approached me with a story idea of his own. It seemed that a New Jersey hospital was preparing to do an unprecedented operation on a man who had been born without eyes.

"What is this?" I asked in exasperation. "Am I being reassigned to the weird deformities beat?"

Almost as soon as I had the sentence out of my mouth, I realized that it was time to reassess myself both as a reporter and as a human being. As a journalist I was totally fed up with writing stories about other people's misfortunes. But as a human being I was alarmed that I was losing my feeling for these same miseries. To me, the deepest human tragedy had become just another routine story. It frightened me.

For the next few days I dwelled upon the changes that had occurred in my personality during the previous ten years. I thought about my mother and Thomas Hamilton and the flood victims in Wilkes-Barre. I thought about the National Spelling Bee and L. Patrick Gray and the Miss America Pageant. I thought about Donald Sutherland and Dick Clark and Michael Abt. And the more I thought, the more I realized that I had to think some more.

Because I obviously needed more time to reflect, I decided to lay plans for two possible courses of action: I applied for law school at the University of San Francisco, and I applied for a Nieman Fellowship at Harvard University, which is a special one-year program of study for journalists. Then I waited.

At the time it was difficult to explain my growing malaise to anyone outside of the newspaper business. There I was, working for a Pulitzer Prize-winning newspaper, making four times the money I had ever dreamed possible, traveling all over the country. And yet I wasn't happy.

One of the few nonjournalists who understood was Paul Specht, a friend since college days. A few years earlier Paul had noticed that I had become completely enveloped by my image as a newspaper reporter. It was so bad, in fact, that Paul and his wife, Carol, made a bet with me one night that I couldn't make it through a party without mentioning my job.

I did, but it was difficult. For all of my adult life, I had identified myself as Kathy Begley, Staff Writer. I wasn't nearly so secure as Kathy Begley, Human Being.

My extreme dependence on my job also was brought home to me by Ed Williames, one of the best friends anyone ever had. Eddie frequently telephoned me at the office.

"Are you on deadbeat?" he would joke, deliberately mistaking the word for deadline.

"Yeah," I would reply, often not even taking time out to laugh at his humor. "I'll call you back in an hour."

There was little doubt that for a long time I had sacrificed much of my personal life and many of my friends in order to succeed in my job. But I still couldn't decide what to do about it.

As it turned out, I didn't have much of a decision to make. As I was muddling over alternatives in my mind, I received acceptance from the University of San Francisco Law School. Studying law was something I had wanted to do for a long time. I decided to go there.

The day after I resigned from the *Inquirer*, I received a letter from the Nieman organization inviting me to Cambridge for an interview. But by then my decision to leave journalism for at least three years was firm. Or so I believed.

Almost everyone thought I had gone completely crazy. I was, after all, leaving newspaper work at the height of its prestige and allure. I was, without question, throwing away a decade of experience. I was, no doubt, entering an unknown and unrelated field.

All of my critics were right. I didn't present any arguments. I just knew that law school, at this particular time in my life, was right for me.

The day after I resigned, Gene Roberts walked up to me in the city room and told me he was sorry I was leaving. I told him I was too.

"But, you know, Gene," I said. "If I go to law school, I can still be a reporter. But if I don't, I can never be a lawyer."

On my last day at the *Inquirer* Gene gave me a letter of recommendation that made me feel happy and sad at the same time. It said, in part:

> She is an unusually gifted writer and demonstrated that again and again. She left the *Inquirer* because she decided to go to law school. The *Inquirer* regarded this decision as a good one for the legal profession but a bad one for journalism.

Because I feel uncomfortable during long good-byes, I deliberately packed up my files and notebooks on a

Saturday, when few reporters or editors are around. It was almost five years to the day that I first joined the *Inquirer* staff.

After gathering up my motley collection of bent paper clips, stretched rubber bands, and dog-eared books, I headed for the elevator that would carry me down from the fifth floor newsroom for the last time. I am happy to say that I did not remain entirely objective about my own departure.

I cried.

Epilogue

During my first semester at law school, I discovered something about myself that I had suspected for a long time: I am a journalism junkie. Try as I might to shake the writing habit and devote myself totally to my legal studies, I found that I greatly missed the day-to-day adventures of newspaper life.

So in early 1977, I decided to accept a reporting job at the Chicago *Daily News* that promises to be as exciting as my former position at the *Inquirer.* I now plan to finish law school at an evening program in Chicago.

The intervening months have taught me a great deal about my commitment as a reporter and as a writer. To be sure, many people would view my feelings about journalism as an addiction. But it's one I can't seem to give up. So, frankly, I'm going to stop trying.

I may as well face the facts. I'm hooked.

THE AUTHOR

Kathleen A. Begley first decided she wanted to be a writer in third grade, when the teacher tacked her composition about the circus on the bulletin board. Little did it matter that Kathy never had been to the circus. What mattered was that the class applauded—and she liked the sound.

Years passed before Kathy made another major decision: she would become a journalist. By that time she was attending Notre Dame High School in Moylan, Pennsylvania. She joined the staff of the high-school newspaper and came under the influence of a worldly-wise nun, Sister Marie Dolores. As long-suffering as she was wise, Sister Marie Dolores steered Kathy in good directions.

We next find our heroine working as a copygirl for the Delaware County *Daily Times* in Chester, Pennsylvania. But to learn more about what happened to her you really must read her first book, *Deadline. . . .*

WATERLOO HIGH SCHOOL
1464 Industry Rd.
Atwater, Ohio 44201

M